FORGIV

IS

DIVINE

Five steps to forgiveness

Bright Osei Twumasi

Bright Osei Twumasi • 2023

ISBN: 978-1-916686-00-7 (Paperback)
ISBN: 978-1-916686-01-4 (Ebook)

British Library Cataloguing in Publication Data.
A catalogue record for this book is available from the British Library.

First Edition. June 30, 2023.

Published by Bright Osei Twumasi.
Unit 121419, PO Box 6945, London, W1A 6US
Email: oseibright@yahoo.com
Web: www.oseibright.com

Contents

Contents

Foreword

As the senior minister of Trinity Baptist Church, New Addington London, I was fortunate and privileged to have had Dr Bright Osei Twumasi on our leadership team. With his Christian and educational background and experience, he became a great asset to the Church and was appointed as a Bible study teacher and a lay preacher. In 2016-2017, I assigned a preaching series on forgiveness to Bright, to be delivered on specific Sundays.

The topic was treated with great commitment, dedication, and passion. I was impressed by the impact of the series and suggested he should write a book on the topic. When Bright later asked me to suggest a title for the book, I proposed *forgiveness is divine*—which is meant to emphasize the fact that forgiveness is rooted in God himself, a concept which Bright has impressively explored in this book.

I can confidently say Bright has written a book that reflects his personal life experiences and his willingness to obey the promptings of the Holy Spirit as a child of God. His faith in God and love for the word of God have served as a backbone to enable him to stand the numerous trials, disappointments and temptations of life.

The book is an inspirational and practical guide for every child of God who desires to follow the example of God on forgiveness. The book gives insight into the processes adopted by God in dealing with his own people in terms of forgiveness, and his requirements towards us. Bright traces God's own experience of forgiveness in his ultimate plan of salvation, and then apply the lessons to explain God's requirements of forgiveness to the Church.

I wholly recommend this book to any Christian who seeks to live their life by the principles and culture of God. Reading this book would serve as a good starting point as far as true forgiveness is concerned.

Reverend Sampson Dankyi
Senior Minister
Trinity Baptist Church
New Addington, London

Preface

This book was conceived during my role as a Sunday School teacher and lay preacher at Trinity Baptist Church, New Addington, London (2016-2018). During this time, I was assigned a teaching series on Forgiveness by Pastor Sampson Dankyi to be delivered on specified Sundays. The ideas of this book were initially conceived during the delivery of the series.

The motivation for the book arose from two primary Scriptures:

> "This is the covenant I will make with the people of Israel after that time," declares the LORD .... "I will forgive their wickedness and will remember their sins no more." (Jer 31:33-34)

> Follow God's example, therefore, as dearly loved children and walk in the way of love, just as Christ loved us and gave himself up for us as a fragrant offering and sacrifice to God. (Eph 5:1-2)

The first Scripture describes the promise of God to forgive sin and remember no more in the New Covenant.

The idea of God promising to forgive and no longer re-member sin sparked my search to understand the mean-ing, context and implication of this key promise of for-giveness. My journey led me to prayerfully examine for-giveness under the Old Covenant, and how it would be different in the New Covenant due to the above promise of God. I came to realise that, as part of his overall plan of salvation, God, through Christ, accomplished five steps or stages in forgiveness: remembering our sins no more, not taking vengeance against us, reconciling us to himself, doing good and praying for us.

The second Scripture instructs us to follow the exam-ple of God as his dearly loved children. When applied to forgiveness, this means walking the same path God followed in forgiving us. Thus, for each of the five stages of forgiveness identified above, we learn how God himself took the step, and how he requires all Christians to follow him in this journey. In other words, we learn from the ex-amples of God, and apply the lessons to his instructions for us.

It is worth noting that some of the topics covered in this book, such as reconciliation, are central themes in Christianity on which whole books have been written by other authors. The treatment of these topics in this book focuses on their overall relation to forgiveness, and no further. Thus, I have avoided digressing from my central theme of forgiveness.

It is my humble and sincere prayer that this book may be used in the service of God to further his purposes.

The book would not have reached a successful com-pletion without the support and encouragement of Pas-tor Dankyi and members of Trinity Baptist Church. The Church provided the platform to share and refine some of the ideas in this book, and I am grateful for the opportunity. Some members of the Church provided perspectives on some of the topics. In particular, my thanks go to brother Oti Festus and the late Madam Lydia Omenyo who made specific suggestions.

My sincere gratitude also goes to Elder Isaac Mensah of the Church of Pentecost, Nottingham, United Kingdom. Isaac has been a friend and a brother in the Lord for over 20 years. Some of the ideas of this book have been debated through our numerous discussions. Isaac also provided a review of the manuscript, leading to corrections and valuable suggestions for improvement.

Finally, my thanks go to Dr Akwasi Darko Ampem for proofreading the book and providing corrections, suggestions or insights.

Bright Osei Twumasi
London, June 2023.

Chapter 1

Introduction

This book discusses the principles of Christian forgiveness. We conceive of forgiveness as a five-stage process or journey, symbolized by climbing a ladder where each stage or step is higher than the previous one. The journey is complete when one arrives at the final stage of the process.

Christian forgiveness is a divine process, that is, forgiveness is rooted in God's own journey from remembering and punishing past sins in the Old Covenant to absolute forgiveness in the New Covenant. God himself has already taken each of the five steps on this journey of forgiveness, providing the mandate and the example for Christians. He does not stand aside and point to the way, rather, he commands us to follow in his footsteps, in moving from unforgiveness to absolute forgiveness.

The five steps on the journey of forgiveness are:

1. **Remember no more**: forgive and forget, do not dwell on the offence or allow it to have an impact on your relationships.

2. **Do not take revenge**: do not retaliate, pay back or take any form of vengeance against the offender.

3. **Reconcile with the offender**: make every effort to restore the previous relationship destroyed by the offence.

4. **Do good to the offender**: demonstrate kindness towards the offender.

5. **Pray for the offender**: intercede on behalf of the offender for forgiveness and reconciliation by God.

The general format followed in this book is: for each step on the journey of forgiveness, we learn how God himself took the step, and how he requires all Christians to follow him in this journey. The chapters are organised as follows.

Chapter 2 discusses the first step: *Remember no more.* In the Old Testament, God was unable or unwilling to permanently forgive sin, without the atonement of Christ. He remembered and punished the current generation for the sins of the past, up to four generations. The reason why God was morally unable or unwilling to permanently forgive is discussed, as well as the implications.

Thankfully, God promised a New Covenant in which he would forgive our sins and remember them no more. This promise was fulfilled in the atonement of Christ, which allowed God to permanently forgive all those who appeal to Christ for salvation. In the New Covenant, God simply *forgets* the past when he forgives a person who has placed their faith in Christ. That is, from the moment of forgiveness, God regards the person as a new creation, and their sinful past has no bearing on his relationship with them. This is true forgiveness, and the foundation of Christian principles of forgiveness. God requires us to follow his footstep in forgiving those who offend us and remember their sin no more.

Chapter 3 discusses the second step: *Do not take revenge.* The vengeance of God in the Old Testament is described: his vengeance was often severe, immediate and collective in application. To a large extent, the covenant he established with Israel was based on the principles of vengeance, typified by "an for an eye" laws.

In the New Covenant, God moved away from those old principles of vengeance and established new principles of grace and forgiveness. God himself followed the new principles when he forgave us, declaring no condemnation for those who have appealed to Christ for salvation. He similarly commands Christians to extend the same treatment to others and shun revenge or any form of retaliatory action against those who offend us. Rather than taking revenge, we can appeal to God who has said it is his prerogative to exercise vengeance as he sees fit. We can also appeal to the governing authorities for justice.

Chapter 4 discusses the third step: *Reconcile with the offender.* That is, restoring the previous relationship which has been destroyed by the offence. As usual we begin with the example of God, who after forgetting our sins also reconciled us to himself. In order to unravel the mystery of the reconciliation of mankind to God, the relationship man had with God prior to the Fall is reviewed. Man was in perfect harmony with God, his creation and within the faculties of his spirit and soul.

Unfortunately, the Fall happened, and mankind was plunged into a state of sinfulness and darkness. Through the atonement of Christ, God reconciled mankind to himself, and restored the previous relationship and privileges that were lost. To help achieve his ultimate aim of reconciling all things to himself, God committed to Christians the "ministry of reconciliation." Christians are both witnesses and agents of God, commanded to spread the message of reconciliation in the world. God expects Christians to reconcile with those who offend them, as far as it is within their power. However, the Scriptures acknowledge that reconciliation is not always possible and provide a framework for Christians to follow in such cases.

Chapter 5 discusses the fourth step: *Do good to the offender.* God demonstrated his love and goodness towards us in the atonement of Christ. Furthermore, as part of the atonement, he "blessed us in the heavenly realms with every spiritual blessing in Christ."[1] The key blessings are discussed, including unlimited forgiveness, the gifts of the Holy Spirit and healing of diseases. All these blessings have been made possible by the atonement of Christ, who died for us while we were still enemies of God. God expects us to follow his example and exercise the same goodness towards those who offend us. We are commanded to do good to those hate us, and in doing so, we will overcome evil with good and heap burning shame on them, which could ultimately result in their repentance and reconciliation.

Chapter 6 discusses the final step of forgiveness: *Pray for the offender.* This is the ultimate and most glorious step in following God on his journey from unforgiveness to absolute forgiveness. After his death and resurrection, Christ sat at the right hand of God, making intercession for us. We discuss the purpose of Christ's intersession

---

[1] Eph 1:3

and why it is effective. Christ commands us to follow his example by praying for those who offend us. Anyone who genuinely takes this step has truly followed God and completed the journey of divine forgiveness.

Chapter 2

Remember no more

Before the actual institution of the New Covenant,[1] God predicted through prophet Jeremiah:

> "This is the covenant I will make with the people of Israel after that time," declares the LORD. "I will put my law in their minds and write it on their hearts. I will be their God, and they will be my people. No longer will they teach their neighbor, or say to one another, 'Know the LORD,' because they will all know me, from the least of them to the greatest," declares the LORD. "For I will forgive their wickedness and will remember their sins no more." (Jer 31:33-34)

In the Scripture above, God predicted that a time was coming when he would establish a new covenant with the people. In this New Covenant, several principles would

---

[1] A covenant is a pact, treaty, alliance, or agreement between two parties of equal or of unequal authority. [holman]

be operated by God, including writing his laws on their hearts. At the end of the list, God declared: "I will forgive their wickedness and will remember their sins no more." This is the key principle we will be focusing on in this Chapter. The statement implies God did not permanently forgive, and remembered sin, under the Old Covenant. This precondition is required for the statement to make sense. To "remember no more" implies that prior to the institution of the New Covenant, God remembered sin.

In the sections that follow, we will explore the meaning, implication and the reason why God could not permanently forgive sin under the Old Covenant.

2.1   How God remembered sin

If God did not permanently forgive sin under the Old Covenant, in what sense did he remember those sins? The following Scripture will help answer this question:

> And he [God] passed in front of Moses, proclaiming, "The LORD, the LORD, the compassionate and gracious God, slow to anger, abounding in love and faithfulness, maintaining love to thousands, and forgiving wickedness, rebellion and sin. Yet he does not leave the guilty unpunished; he punishes the children and their children for the sin of the parents to the third and fourth generation." (Exo 34:6-7; See also Num 14:18; Deut 5:8-10)

In the background to the above passage, God had called

Moses to Mount Sinai to announce the Ten Command-
ments for the people of Israel. Moses spent 40 days with
God on the mountain. The people became restless and
pressured Aaron into building an idol to lead them, thus
totally abandoning the God who had just delivered them
from slavery in Egypt.[2]

God threatened to destroy the entire people because
of their sin. However, Moses earnestly interceded for
them, even telling God "please forgive their sin—but if
not, then blot me out of the book you have written."[3] In
the end, Moses' intersection prevailed over God, having
obtained great favour, even asking to see God's face. God
said Moses could not see his face, but agreed to show his
rear. God then passed by Moses, proclaiming his own
nature in the passage quoted above.

The list of attributes revealed by God himself can be
arranged into two overlapping circles, namely, the circle
of Unforgiveness and the circle of Grace and Forgiveness,
as shown in Figure 2.1.

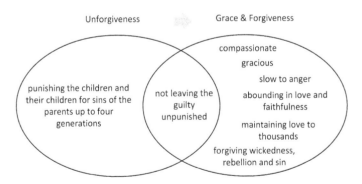

Figure 2.1: The circles of forgiveness and unforgiveness

Consider the statement "he does not leave the guilty

---

[2] Exo 32   [3] Exo 32:32

unpunished." I have placed this statement on the intersection of Forgiveness and Unforgiveness circles. Who is the guilty? While we might be tempted to think of the guilty as those who commit grave atrocities, as far as God is concerned, there is no difference "for all have sinned and fall short of the glory of God."[4] Consequently, prior to the atonement of Christ, all of mankind were guilty of sin before God.[5] If all have sinned and are guilty before God, then in the Old Covenant, the people did not fully enjoy the grace, mercy, goodness, and other wonderful attributes of God till a permanent solution was found in the New Covenant.

A further step from not leaving the guilty unpunished is "punishing the children and their children for the sins of the parents" up to four generations. This means when God punished sin in the Old Testament, he would also recall the sins committed by past generations, and would punish the current generation for those sins as well. This helps explain why God's punishment of sin in the Old Testament was so severe. Under the Old Covenant, God did not permanently forgive sin. Rather, he recalled and punished current generations for past sins committed by their ancestors.

For example, consider the story of God's punishment of the Amalekites through King Saul. This story is a stark illustration of God punishing the current generation for sins of the past.

> Samuel said to Saul, "I am the one the LORD sent to anoint you king over his people Israel; so listen now to the message from the LORD. This is what the LORD Almighty

---

[4] Rom 3:23   [5] See Section 4.2

says: 'I will punish the Amalekites for what
they did to Israel when they waylaid them as
they came up from Egypt. Now go, attack
the Amalekites and totally destroy all that
belongs to them. Do not spare them; put to
death men and women, children and infants,
cattle and sheep, camels and donkeys.'" (1
Sam 15:1-3)

The Amalekites attacked the Israelites without ap-
parent provocation, as they were travelling during the
Exodus,[6] and were weary and worn out.[7] During that
battle, the Israelites defeated the Amalekites, and God
promised to "blot out the name of Amalek from under
heaven."[8] Thus, in the passage above, approximately 300
years[9] since the Amalekites first attacked Israel, God was
fulfilling this promise by punishing the current generation
for the sins of the past: "I will punish the Amalekites for
what they did to Israel." God remembered the sins of the
past, and punished the current generation with alarming
severity: "put to death men and women, children and
infants, cattle and sheep, camels and donkeys."

It appears that the current generation of the
Amalekites were no better than their ancestors, since
they continued to raid and plunder Israeli cities around
the time of David and Saul.[10] This seems to suggest
that God punished the current generation for the sins
of the past only when they followed in the footsteps
of their ancestors in committing sin. The execution
of the Amalekite king by Samuel seems to confirm
that the severe punishment was not only triggered by

---

[6] Exo 17:8   [7] Deut 25:17-18   [8] Exo 17:14   [9] Estimate based on
[timeline].   [10] 1 Sam 30:1-3

the sins of the past, but also by the atrocities of the current generation. When King Agag was brought before Samuel, he pleaded for mercy. However, Samuel told him: "As your sword has made women childless, so will your mother be childless among women."[11] This confirms that the current leaders of Amalekites were also guilty of grave atrocities. Indeed, this principle is explicitly stated in the following Scriptures:

> Suppose there is a righteous man who does what is just and right ... he will surely live .... Suppose he has a violent son, who sheds blood or does any of these other things ... he is to be put to death; his blood will be on his own head. But suppose this son has a son who sees all the sins his father commits, and though he sees them, he does not do such things ... he will not die for his father's sin; he will surely live. But his father will die for his own sin, because he practiced extortion, robbed his brother and did what was wrong among his people. (Eze 18:5-18)

From the above Scripture, a son who followed in the footsteps of his father in committing evil would bear the punishment his own sins, and might also be punished for his father's sins as well. However, a son who did right would not be held responsible for his father's sins. Further, when the primary Scripture under discussion[12] appears in Deuteronomy, a clarification is added:

> I, the LORD your God, am a jealous God, punishing the children for the sin of the parents to the third and fourth generation *of*

---

[11] 1 Sam 15:33   [12] Exo 34:6-7

those who hate me. [emphasis added] (Deut 5:9)

The expression "of those who hate me" suggests the principle of God punishing children for the sin of their parents was primarily carried out on those who hated God and refused to submit to his moral requirements.

However, it should be stated that the principle of God collectively punishing the current generation for the sins of their ancestors was generally held under the Old Covenant. For example, in the punishment of the Amalekites, while their past and current leaders might have been guilty of atrocities, could it really be the case that not a single Amalekite was opposed to their leaders? And how could "children and infants" be held morally responsible for the sins of the adults? Jesus even said: "Let the little children come to me, and do not hinder them, for the kingdom of God belongs to such as these."[13] Thus, Jesus confirmed that children and infants are not moral agents. How then could God command King Saul to kill children, infants and animals?

The answer, I believe, lies in God's inability or unwillingness to permanently forgive sin without the atonement of Christ. This meant that he not only punished the current generation collectively for their own sin, but also for sins of their ancestors. Noah's flood,[14] Sodom and Gomorrah,[15] Uzzah[16] and Achan[17]—are all clear examples of God remembering and punishing sins collectively and severely under the Old Covenant. The reason why sin could not be forgiven without Christ's atonement has been discussed in Section 2.2.

---

[13] Mark 10:14   [14] Gen 7   [15] Gen 19   [16] 2 Sam 6   [17] Josh 7

The following Scriptures provide further confirmation of the principle of God remembering and punishing past sins under the Old Covenant.

> Do not hold against us the sins of past generations. (Psa 79:8)

> May the iniquity of his fathers be remembered before the LORD; may the sin of his mother never be blotted out. (Psa 109:14)

> Do not remember the sins of my youth and my rebellious ways; according to your love remember me, for you, LORD, are good. (Psa 25:7)

> God will remember their wickedness and punish them for their sins. (Hos 9:9)

> Whenever I would heal Israel, the sins of Ephraim are exposed and the crimes of Samaria revealed .... Their sins engulf them; they are always before me. (Hos 7:1-2)

2.2   Why God could not forgive

When God created life, he established a key principle on forgiveness, namely:

> In fact, the law requires that nearly everything be cleansed with blood, and without the shedding of blood there is no forgiveness. (Heb 9:22)

For the life of a creature is in the blood,
and I have given it to you to make atonement
for yourselves on the altar; it is the blood that
makes atonement for one's life. (Lev 17:11)

The implication of the above principle is that sin could not be forgiven without the shedding of blood to make atonement for the sin. The life or soul of a living being resides in their blood. Consequently, when the blood is shed on the sacrificial altar, this life atones and intercedes on behalf of the sinner for forgiveness by God.

It is important to understand the implication of the above principle. By establishing the principle of "no forgiveness without atonement by blood," God bound himself to that principle. That is, God was not able or willing to forgive sin without atonement by blood. The reason why God established this principle of forgiveness is not evident in the Scriptures.

Under the Old Covenant, the blood of animals was used for the atonement of sin. Detailed and specific prescriptions were established for animal sacrifices for various sins.[18] The animals used for atoning sacrifice were required to be unblemished, signifying innocence and sinlessness.[19] Essentially, the sin of the guilty party was transferred unto the sacrificial animal whose blood was then shed to make atonement for the sinner.

In the New Covenant, we learn that animal sacrifices were only a temporary feature of the ultimate plan of God to provide a permanent solution to sin:

For the law, having a shadow of the good
things to come, and not the very image of the

---

[18] Lev 1-16   [19] Deut 17:1; Lev 22:17-25

> things, can never with these same sacrifices,
> which they offer continually year by year,
> make those who approach perfect. For then
> would they not have ceased to be offered?
> For the worshipers, once purified, would have
> had no more consciousness of sins. But in
> those sacrifices there is a reminder of sins
> every year. For it is not possible that the
> blood of bulls and goats could take away
> sins. (Heb 10:1-4 NKJV)

The various elements of the plan of God now seem clearer. Essentially, when mankind sinned in the Fall,[20] God knew that the only way to permanently solve the problem of sin was through the perfect blood of Christ. For reasons known only to God, Christ did not fulfil the purpose of God sooner following the Fall—it would take approximately 4,000 years for the Son of God to be manifest in the flesh.[21] In the interim, God provided a temporary cover for sin, in the form of animal sacrifices, under the Old Covenant. Animal sacrifices were designed to provide a temporary reprieve from the wrath of God against sin, till the incarnation of Christ. Since it is impossible for the blood of animals to permanently take away sin, these sacrifices had to be repeated yearly. Notwithstanding the sacrifices, God still remembered the sins and the people felt guilty for their sins after the sacrifices.

We can now set the promise of the New Covenant in the proper context when God says: "I will forgive their

---

[20] See Section 4.2   [21] The Scriptures reveal the function of the Old Covenant and the Law in fulfilling God's purpose, as discussed in Section 2.3. However, the reason behind the actual timing of Christ's incarnation is not evident.

wickedness and will remember their sins no more." That is, in the New Covenant, I will provide an absolute solution for sin through the blood of my Son, which will allow me to permanently forgive sin and remember no more.

> For if there had been nothing wrong with that first covenant, no place would have been sought for another. But God found fault with the people and said: "The days are coming, declares the Lord, when I will make a new covenant with the people of Israel .... I will forgive their wickedness and will remember their sins no more." (Heb 8:7-12)

Thus, the key characteristic of the New Covenant is that forgiveness is absolute and permanent, i.e. there is no longer a "reminder of sin" with God or "guilt of sin" for those who have obtained forgiveness. This has been made possible by the atoning sacrifice of Christ, the Lamb of God who was slaughtered for our sins.

2.3 Need for the New Covenant

As the Scriptures state: "If there had been nothing wrong with that first covenant, no place would have been sought for another."[22] God, finding fault with the first covenant, promised a new covenant. The New Covenant is designed to supersede the faulty Old Covenant, to provide a better and permanent solution for the problem of sin. In the following paragraphs, the key weaknesses of the Old Covenant have been summarised.

---

[22] Heb 8:7

The fundamental weakness of the Old Covenant has already been discussed, i.e. forgiveness of sin was temporary, animal sacrifices could not permanently take away sin, God remembered sin and the people felt guilty for their sins after those sacrifices. In addition, the vehicle by which the Old Covenant was implemented (i.e. the Law) was weak and could not achieve the desired purpose of God. In his epistles, Paul discussed in greater detail the weaknesses of the Old Covenant Law (henceforth referred to as "the Law"). Paul asks: "What purpose then does the law serve?"[23] The key functions and weaknesses of the Law are summarized below.

First, the Law "was added because of transgressions until the Seed to whom the promise referred had come."[24] Notice the term *added*. The Law was not originally intended to give deliverance from sin, neither could it impart life: for if salvation came from the Law, there would have been no need for faith.[25] But the Scripture says the Law was added because of transgression, till the fullness of time when Christ by his atonement would condemn sin in the flesh and reconcile mankind to God. Hence, the Law was intended to restrain mankind from the commission of sin, to keep the manifestation of evil within bounds till the appearance of Christ.

Second, the Law was given to define and reveal sin; that is, "through the law we become conscious of our sin."[26] The Law brings to man the full knowledge of sin: "I would not have known what sin was had it not been for the law."[27]

Third, not only does the Law bring the knowledge of sin, it also brings its doom: "because the law brings

---

[23] Gal 3:19 NKJV   [24] Gal 3:19   [25] Gal 3:18   [26] Rom 3:20   [27] Rom 7:7

wrath. And where there is no law there is no transgression."[28] There is a "curse of the law" which comes upon all who violate it.[29]

Fourth, the Law stimulates sin and was given for that purpose: "the law was brought in so that the trespass might increase."[30] The Law itself is "holy, and the commandment is holy, righteous and good."[31] However, sin took advantage of the Law and produced death in the people.[32] Thus, the Law was weakened by the flesh,[33] and could not give life but led to only despair: "What a wretched man I am! Who will rescue me from this body that is subject to death?"[34]

Fifth, the Law was designed as guardian to lead and point mankind to Christ. "Before the coming of this faith, we were held in custody under the law, locked up until the faith that was to come would be revealed. So the law was our guardian until Christ came that we might be justified by faith."[35] The Law had "only a shadow of the good things that are coming—not the realities themselves."[36] The tabernacle, ceremonies, sabbaths, sacrifices, etc., all foreshadowed Christ and his ministry.

The foregoing discussion summarizes the key weaknesses of the Old Covenant and the Law. These weaknesses meant that the Old Covenant could not provide a permanent solution to the problem of sin, thus necessitating the New Covenant. "For if a law had been given that could impart life, then righteousness would certainly have come by the law."[37]

---

[28] Rom 4:15   [29] Gal 3:10   [30] Rom 5:20   [31] Rom 7:12   [32] Rom 7:7-12   [33] Rom 8:3   [34] Rom 7:24   [35] Gal 3:23-24   [36] Heb 10:1   [37] Gal 3:21

2.4   Christ, God's solution to sin

As has been stated repeatedly, God promised permanent forgiveness in the New Covenant. This promise was fulfilled in the sacrifice of his Son, Jesus Christ, through whom he made atonement for the sins of the world. The atonement of Christ allowed God to permanently forgive sin and remember no more. A full picture is given in Hebrews chapter 10.

> The law is only a shadow of the good things that are coming—not the realities themselves. For this reason it can never, by the same sacrifices repeated endlessly year after year, make perfect those who draw near to worship. Otherwise, would they not have stopped being offered? For the worshipers would have been cleansed once for all, and would no longer have felt guilty for their sins. But those sacrifices are an annual reminder of sins. It is impossible for the blood of bulls and goats to take away sins.

> Therefore, when Christ came into the world, he said: "Sacrifices and offerings, burnt offerings and sin offerings you did not desire, nor were you pleased with them"—though they were offered in accordance with the law. Then he said, "Here I am, I have come to do your will." He sets aside the first to establish the second. And by that will, we have been made holy through the sacrifice of the body of Jesus Christ once for all .... For by one sacrifice he has made perfect forever those

who are being made holy.

The Holy Spirit also testifies to us about this .... "This is the covenant I will make with them after that time, says the Lord .... Their sins and lawless acts I will remember no more." And where these have been forgiven, sacrifice for sin is no longer necessary. (Heb 10:1-18)

The foregoing Scripture needs no commentary. Christ came to fulfil the promise of God, to provide a permanent solution to the problem of sin.

Do not think that I have come to abolish the Law or the Prophets; I have not come to abolish them but to fulfill them. (Matt 5:17)

Christ is the culmination of the law so that there may be righteousness for everyone who believes. (Rom 10:4)

The atoning sacrifice of Christ is described as perfect, once-for-all, eternal redemption, one sacrifice for sins, able to put away sin forever and purify our guilty conscience.[38] Christ's atonement allowed God to absolve and justify the guilty. We saw previously how God would not let the guilty go unpunished and how all have sinned and fall short of the glory of God.[39] How then could God absolve and justify guilty sinners? He found the answer in Christ, the sacrificial Lamb. By transferring the sins of mankind onto Christ (the Substitute), and sacrificing him in our place, God was able to forgive and justify sinners who repent and place their faith in Christ. This is the central message of the Gospel.

---

[38] Heb 10:10,12,14; 7:27; 9:24-28; 1 Pet 3:18   [39] See Section 2.1

Surely he took up our pain and bore our suffering, yet we considered him punished by God, stricken by him, and afflicted. But he was pierced for our transgressions, he was crushed for our iniquities; the punishment that brought us peace was on him, and by his wounds we are healed. We all, like sheep, have gone astray, each of us has turned to our own way; and the LORD has laid on him the iniquity of us all. (Isa 53:4-6)

For Christ also suffered once for sins, the righteous for the unrighteous, to bring you to God. He was put to death in the body but made alive in the Spirit. (1 Pet 3:18)

"He himself bore our sins" in his body on the cross, so that we might die to sins and live for righteousness; "by his wounds you have been healed." (1 Pet 2:24)

For all have sinned and fall short of the glory of God, and all are justified freely by his grace through the redemption that came by Christ Jesus. God presented Christ as a sacrifice of atonement, through the shedding of his blood—to be received by faith. He did this to demonstrate his righteousness, because in his forbearance he had left the sins committed beforehand unpunished—he did it to demonstrate his righteousness at the present time, so as to be just and the one who justifies those who have faith in Jesus. (Rom 3:23-26)

In Christ, God was able to fulfil the demands of justice and at the same time absolve the guilty sinner. Justice demanded that the penalty of sin, which is death,[40] must be paid. By transferring our sins onto Christ and sacrificing him, God fully paid that penalty. The sinner, by placing their faith in Christ, appeals to the atonement for salvation. This allows God to justify him, making God just and the justifier of those who have faith in Christ. In other words, in justifying the sinner, God remains just—impartial, righteous and blameless. "If we confess our sins, he is faithful and just and will forgive us our sins and purify us from all unrighteousness."[41] In other words, when the sinner confesses their sin by faith in Christ, not only will God be faithful to his promise to forgive and remember no more, he will also be just in doing so.

As the psalmist predicted:

> Surely his salvation is near those who fear him, that his glory may dwell in our land. Love and faithfulness meet together; righteousness and peace kiss each other. (Psa 85:9-10)

That is, by virtue of his atonement, Christ became the meeting point where the righteousness and peace of God embraced, making God just and the justifier of those who believe in Christ.

In Christ, the following Scriptures find their full fulfilment:

> As far as the east is from the west, so far has he removed our transgressions from us. (Psa 103:12)

---

[40] Rom 6:23 [41] 1 John 1:9

> Though your sins are like scarlet, they shall be as white as snow; though they are red as crimson, they shall be like wool. (Isa 1:18)

> I have swept away your offenses like a cloud, your sins like the morning mist. (Isa 44:22)

> You have put all my sins behind your back. (Isa 38:17)

The foregoing Scriptures say the same thing—that, in the New Covenant, once God forgives sin, he does not remember it any more. In other words, from the point of forgiveness, our past matters no more with God. Ezekiel explains the principle more clearly:

> But if a wicked person turns away from all the sins they have committed and keeps all my decrees and does what is just and right, that person will surely live; they will not die. None of the offenses they have committed will be remembered against them. Because of the righteous things they have done, they will live. (Eze 18:21-22)

In the New Covenant, God simply *forgets* the past when he forgives the one who has placed their faith in Christ. Of course, this is figurative language—God by nature has perfect knowledge and cannot literally forget the past. The meaning is: from the very moment God forgives a person, their past has absolutely no impact on God's relationship with them. As Ezekiel predicted—none of the offences they have committed will be remembered against them. As far as God is concerned, the person is a "new creation"—the old person has died and a new person has been created in God's righteous and holy image. This is absolute forgiveness.

> Therefore, if anyone is in Christ, he is a new creation; old things have passed away; behold, all things have become new. (2 Cor 5:17 NKJV)

> I have been crucified with Christ and I no longer live, but Christ lives in me. The life I now live in the body, I live by faith in the Son of God, who loved me and gave himself for me. (Gal 2:20)

> Put on the new self, created to be like God in true righteousness and holiness. (Eph 4:24)

The converse principle also holds—

> But if a righteous person turns from their righteousness and commits sin and does the same detestable things the wicked person does, will they live? None of the righteous things that person has done will be remembered. Because of the unfaithfulness they are guilty of and because of the sins they have committed, they will die. (Eze 18:24)

It is worth noting that righteousness means "right standing with God" (i.e. justification), which in the New Covenant comes by active faith in Christ. Thus, this

principle implies that if one abandons their faith in Christ
(i.e. apostasies), they will be lost. In other words, the
passage is not describing the occasional sin committed
by Christians, which once confessed are forgiven;[42] but
rather a total abandonment of the Faith. Ezekiel gave
further clarification:

> If I tell a righteous person that they will
> surely live, but then they trust in their righ-
> teousness and do evil, none of the righteous
> things that person has done will be remem-
> bered; they will die for the evil they have
> done. (Eze 33:13)

The expression "they trust in their righteousness and
do evil" indicates a reliance on one's own strength and
past morality for salvation, rather than active faith in
Christ. As Paul warns, "they were broken off because of
unbelief, and you stand by faith. Do not be arrogant,
but tremble."[43] Also, "the just shall live by faith; But if
anyone draws back [their faith], My soul has no pleasure
in him."[44]

Returning to forgiveness, a direct consequence of God
forgetting past sins is that the current generation will
no longer be punished for the sins of past generations.
Ezekiel described it as follows:

> The one who sins is the one who will die.
> The child will not share the guilt of the par-
> ent, nor will the parent share the guilt of the
> child. The righteousness of the righteous will
> be credited to them, and the wickedness of

---

[42] 1 John 1:9   [43] Rom 11:20   [44] Heb 10:38 NKJV

the wicked will be charged against them. (Eze
18:20)

That is, in the New Covenant, everyone shall be
judged by God in accordance with their own ways. No
one will be responsible for the sins of another, as further
confirmed by the following Scriptures.

The word of the LORD came to me:
"What do you people mean by quoting
this proverb about the land of Israel: 'The
parents eat sour grapes, and the children's
teeth are set on edge'? As surely as I live,
declares the Sovereign LORD, you will no
longer quote this proverb in Israel. (Eze
18:1-3)

God "will repay each person according to
what they have done." (Rom 2:6)

For the Son of Man is going to come in
his Father's glory with his angels, and then
he will reward each person according to what
they have done. (Matt 16:27)

And I saw the dead, great and small,
standing before the throne, and books were
opened .... The dead were judged according
to what they had done as recorded in the
books. (Rev 20:12)

2.5   Forgive and forget

We have seen how God through his prophets began to
tell the people about the New Covenant he was going

to establish at the appointed time, and the new principles he was going to operate. The people were so accustomed to unforgiveness they could not understand the fairness of the new principles. When God declared that the son shall no longer be responsible for the sins of the father, the people asked: "Why does the son not share the guilt of his father?"[45] When God declared that the righteousness or wickedness of a person shall be upon only themselves, the people exclaimed "the way of the Lord is not just."[46] It is quite amazing how unforgiveness was so ingrained in their consciousness that they were baffled by the new principles. They were so accustomed to the Old Covenant principle of "an eye for an eye" that the new principles seemed alien to them. Nevertheless, God was making a new covenant with new principles, and the people must change their mindset, and follow God in this journey from unforgiveness to absolute forgiveness. They must be ready to say with God: "I will forgive and remember no more." This is the very first step in that journey.

The foundation of Christian forgiveness is God's own journey from unforgiveness to absolute forgiveness, from remembering and punishing past sins to total forgetfulness of sin. He now requires us to follow his footsteps, to forgive our neighbours and remember their sin no more. To borrow the words of Peter, in times of ignorance God overlooked, but now he commands everyone to forgive and forget. This is the first principle of forgiveness. For Christians under the New Covenant, the requirement to forgive and forget is absolute and emphatic. We forgive our neighbours because God in Christ forgave us. We

---

[45] Eze 18:19   [46] Eze 18:25; 29; 33:17

remember their sin no more because God in Christ remember our own sins no more, once confessed. Let us take that first step, and say with God, I will forgive and remember no more.

The Scriptures command us:

> Follow God's example, therefore, as dearly loved children and walk in the way of love, just as Christ loved us and gave himself up for us as a fragrant offering and sacrifice to God. (Eph 5:1-2)

This means we are to follow the footsteps of God in forgiving others and remembering their offences no more. As mentioned in Section 2.4, *forgetting* someone's offence is figurative language. The human mind cannot literally forget something voluntarily or simply by willing. Forgetting means choosing not to dwell on the offence: a commitment on our part to make every effort to prevent the offence from impacting our relationship with the offender. By doing so, we are essentially treating the person as "a new creation" and not as the old person who offended us. In other words, we are following God's example, in moving from unforgiveness to absolute forgiveness. This is the meaning of "forgive and forget."

Chapter 3

Do not take revenge

The previous Chapter laid the foundation of Christian principles of forgiveness. Forgiveness was envisaged as a five-stage journey which began with God himself. The first step, remember no more, was explored in depth, learning about how God fulfilled his promise to remember our sins no more, and how he now requires us to follow his example.

This Chapter discusses the second step, namely, not taking revenge or any kind of retaliatory actions against the offender. This is exactly what God did when he forgave us in Christ, and expects us to extend the same treatment towards those who offend us.

3.1   Old principles of vengeance

In order to appreciate the importance of not taking revenge, we will explore God's attitude to vengeance under the Old Covenant.

A cursory inspection of the Old Testament will reveal

the attitude of God regarding his wrath and vengeance against those who rebelled against his laws. Several examples of God's vengeance were mentioned in the previous Chapter when we discussed God's punishment of past sins. Not only did God punish past sins, but also his vengeance against sin was often immediate, severe and collective in application. This is further discussed in the following subsections.

3.1.1   God's vengeance was immediate

A common theme that occurs throughout the Old Testament is the instant justice meted by God to those who violated his laws. Those who sinned against God were often met with immediate punishment, sometimes instant death penalty.

For example, when the Israelites complained about their food, the fire of the Lord descended and consumed many.[1] When Korah, Dathan, and Abiram staged a rebellion against Moses and God, they were met with an immediate execution at the hand of God, together with 250 other men.[2] When the Israelites complained about their hardships, fire from the Lord immediately consumed some of the outskirts of their camp.[3] When the people of Beth Shemesh looked into the Ark of the Lord, which had come to them from the Philistines, God instantly killed 50,070 of them.[4]

From Genesis to Malachi, the Old Testament is filled with numerous stories of instant punishment meted by

---

[1] Num 11   [2] Num 16:31-35   [3] Num 11:1   [4] 1 Sam 6:19 - A total of 50,070 or 70 were killed depending on the Bible translation. Some translations go for the higher figure (e.g. KJV), while others go for the smaller (e.g. NIV)

God to various people who rebelled against him. Nevertheless, instant retribution did nothing in suppressing the rebellion of mankind against God. This indicates the ineffectiveness of such an approach, which God himself seemed to have highlighted in his promise of the New Covenant.

3.1.2 God's vengeance was severe

Another thing any reader of the Old Testament readily notices is that God's punishment of sin was far more severe, compared to life under the grace of Christ. The aforementioned examples illustrate this fact. The severity of God's vengeance against sin can be plainly seen in many of the books of the Old Testament.

In particular, the Law of God prescribed the death penalty for various offences, including the following:

- Adultery[5]

- Loss of virginity before marriage[6]

- Rape[7]

- Sabbath-breaking[8]

- Cursing a parent[9]

- Persistently disobeying parents[10]

In the New Testament, only a few cases of instant and severe punishment of sin are recorded, such as the punishment of Ananias and Sapphira[11] and the death

---

[5] Lev 20:10   [6] Deut 22:13–21   [7] Deut 22:25–27   [8] Exo 35:2   [9] Exo 21:17   [10] Deut 21:18–21   [11] Acts 5:1-11

of King Herod.[12] Furthermore, Jesus actually prevented the death penalty from being carried out on the woman caught in the act of adultery,[13] signifying a shift from the Old Testament laws of vengeance. Nonetheless, the manifestation of sin and wickedness of mankind under the New Covenant is arguably as much as it was in the Old Covenant (or possibly worse). The key difference between the two dispensations is the appearance of the grace of Christ, which has placated and restrained the wrath of God against sin.

3.1.3   God's vengeance was collective

Collective punishment is punishment imposed on a group for evil acts committed by a certain member or members of that group. As we saw in Section 2.1, collective punishment was a principle generally upheld by God under the Old Covenant. We listed several examples of collective punishment including Noah's flood,[14] Sodom and Gomorrah,[15] the Amalekites,[16] the people of Beth Shemesh,[17] etc. Under this principle, even those who were clearly not moral agents (e.g. infants, children and animals) were nonetheless punished together with the guilty (as in the story of the Amalekites). Furthermore, the unborn descendants of sinners were sometimes cursed or punished.[18]

A sad example of collective punishment involving an innocent baby is the story of David and Bathsheba.[19] King David had sent his army to war, and was strolling on the palace roof in Jerusalem one evening when he saw

---

[12] Acts 12:21-23   [13] John 8:1-11   [14] Gen 6:9-9:17   [15] Gen 19   [16] 1 Sam 15:1-3   [17] 1 Sam 6:19   [18] Deut 28:15,18   [19] 2 Sam 11-12

Bathsheba bathing. Upon enquiring about the woman, he was informed she was the wife of Uriah, one of his soldiers who was at the war front. Nevertheless, he sent for Bathsheba and slept with her. Upon hearing that Bathsheba was pregnant, David sent word to Joab, his general, to dispatch Uriah back to Jerusalem. David's plan was to get Uriah to go home and sleep with his wife, and thereby unwittingly take responsibility for the pregnancy. However, Uriah was an honourable soldier who refused to go home to relax while his comrades were at the war front. When David's plan failed, he sent a sealed letter through Uriah to Joab commanding the latter to place Uriah at the fiercest front of the war and withdraw so he would die.

The events incurred the wrath of God, who sent prophet Nathan to tell David of a story of a rich man who took the only sheep of a poor man despite possessing a large number of sheep. David burned with anger and said: "the man who did this must die!"[20] Nathan told David he was the rich man, and that God would bring calamity upon him and his household as punishment for the evil committed. However, David immediately broke down and repented, saying "I have sinned against the LORD."[21] Nathan replied: "The LORD has taken away your sin. You are not going to die. But because by doing this you have shown utter contempt for the LORD, the son born to you will die."[22] God then struck the child with sickness, and he died seven days later, despite David pleading with God to spare his life.

Due to the principle of collective punishment, an innocent baby who was clearly not a moral agent expe-

---

[20] 2 Sam 12:5   [21] 2 Sam 12:13   [22] 2 Sam 12:13-15

rienced the punishment of the evil committed by King David, who should have known better. It is a relief and wonderful to know that the New Covenant has abolished the principles of collective punishment and children being punished for the sins of their parents.[23]

3.1.4 Laws on vengeance

Perhaps, no verse captures the general principles of vengeance under the Old Covenant better than the phrase "an eye for an eye." This principle of vengeance can be found in following Scripture:

> Anyone who takes the life of a human being is to be put to death. Anyone who takes the life of someone's animal must make restitution—life for life. Anyone who injures their neighbor is to be injured in the same manner: fracture for fracture, eye for eye, tooth for tooth. The one who has inflicted the injury must suffer the same injury. Whoever kills an animal must make restitution, but whoever kills a human being is to be put to death. You are to have the same law for the foreigner and the native-born. I am the LORD your God. (Lev 24:17-22)

The idea behind the above principle is that a person who injures another should be penalized to a similar degree by the courts. Thus, this is system of justice built on revenge. Over time, it is easy to see how such a system could result in the infliction of personal vengeance by the injured party, instead of appealing to the court

---

[23] See Chapter 2

for retribution. It is also easy to see why such a system would not be sustainable in the longer term, and why it was abolished in the New Testament.

> You have heard that it was said, "Eye for eye, and tooth for tooth." But I tell you, do not resist an evil person. If anyone slaps you on the right cheek, turn to them the other cheek also. And if anyone wants to sue you and take your shirt, hand over your coat as well. If anyone forces you to go one mile, go with them two miles. Give to the one who asks you, and do not turn away from the one who wants to borrow from you. (Matt 5:38-42)

3.2 God did not condemn us

When God forgave us in Christ, he did not condemn us, neither did he take any retributive action against us. The following Scriptures clarify this:

> Therefore, there is now no condemnation for those who are in Christ Jesus. (Rom 8:1)

> For God did not send his Son into the world to condemn the world, but to save the world through him. Whoever believes in him is not condemned, but whoever does not believe stands condemned already because they have not believed in the name of God's one and only Son. (John 3:17-18)

> Who then is the one who condemns? No
> one. Christ Jesus who died—more than that,
> who was raised to life—is at the right hand
> of God and is also interceding for us. (Rom
> 8:34)

There is absolutely no condemnation of those who
have placed their faith in Christ; who have obtained absolute and permanent forgiveness. The God who previously would not leave the guilty unpunished under the
Old Covenant has now declared "no condemnation" for
the sake of Christ. As the psalmist puts it, in forgiving
us in Christ, God "does not treat us as our sins deserve or
repay us according to our iniquities."[24] This is true forgiveness! In forgiving us, not only does God forgets our
sins, he also does not punish or take vengeance against
us.

God is so pleased with the efficacy of the atonement
that he challenges anyone who attempts to condemn
those who have put their faith in Christ. "Who then is
the one who condemns?" He offers absolute guarantee to
anyone who surrenders to Christ, that no one would be
able to condemn them.

The absolute forgiveness that came by Christ not only
allowed God to *forget* the past of the guilty sinner who
appeals to the Saviour, but also allows God to revoke
the wrath and vengeance of sin against them. Christ
simply suffered the full punishment of sin on behalf of
the sinner. Hence, there is no more retribution against
the sinner who has appealed to Christ.

---

[24] Psa 103:10

3.3 Do not take revenge

The Scriptural mandate regarding revenge under the New Covenant is absolute and unequivocal—Christians are categorically forbidden from taking revenge against those who offend them.

> Do not take revenge, my dear friends, but leave room for God's wrath, for it is written: "It is mine to avenge; I will repay," says the Lord. (Rom 12:19)

The divine directive is clear—do not take revenge—an absolute prohibition. In other words, taking revenge against an offender is contrary to the principles of the New Covenant and is absolutely prohibited. There are two primary reasons why God prohibits us from taking revenge on those who offend us, discussed in the next sections.

3.3.1 New principles in New Covenant

The first reason why revenge is prohibited under the New Covenant is that God established new principles of forgiveness that supersede the old principles of vengeance. These principles are the five stages of forgiveness which form the basis of this book, as we have previously seen.

The new principles are also applicable to himself—as he has demonstrated in the life, death and ministry of Christ. Thus, God requires all Christians to follow his example and abstain from revenge and any kind of retaliatory action against those who offend them. We are commanded to forgive just as God, through Christ, forgave us. We are prohibited from taking revenge just as

God did not condemn us in Christ. This is such an important principle that Jesus even linked our own forgiveness by God to our willingness to forgive others.

> And forgive us our debts, as we also have forgiven our debtors .... For if you forgive other people when they sin against you, your heavenly Father will also forgive you. But if you do not forgive others their sins, your Father will not forgive your sins. (Matt 6:12-15)

> And when you stand praying, if you hold anything against anyone, forgive them, so that your Father in heaven may forgive you your sins. (Mark 11:25-26)

> Do not condemn, and you will not be condemned. Forgive, and you will be forgiven. (Luke 6:37)

> In anger his master handed him over to the jailers to be tortured, until he should pay back all he owed. "This is how my heavenly Father will treat each of you unless you forgive your brother or sister from your heart." (Matt 18:34-35)

The clear implication of the above Scriptures is that when we fail to forgive others their offences, God will refuse to forgive us our own. Indeed, this is the wider principle embodied in the golden rule: "love your neighbor as yourself"[25] and "do to others what you would have

---

[25] Luke 10:27

them do to you."[26] Do you want God and others to forgive
your offences against them? Then you should be willing
to do the same for others. "For in the same way you
judge others, you will be judged, and with the measure
you use, it will be measured to you."[27]

The aforementioned principles go to the heart of the
doctrine of salvation. Repentance is a prerequisite of
forgiveness and justification by the grace of Christ. And
the Scriptures make it clear that repentance does not stop
at the initial point of salvation. Rather, repentance is a
continual process whereby the Christian obtains pardon
and cleansing from sinful contamination in order to be
preserved towards final redemption at the end of their life
or the second coming of Christ, whichever comes first.

When a sinner appeals to Christ, they obtain salvation by faith in Christ. However, this does not imply that
they become sinless; those in Christ can indeed occasionally fall into sin as they succumb to temptation. As part
of his plan of salvation, God has made provisions to forgive the Christian's sins—conditional on repentance and
confession. The following Scriptures clarify this:

> If we claim to be without sin, we deceive
> ourselves and the truth is not in us. If we
> confess our sins, he is faithful and just and
> will forgive us our sins and purify us from
> all unrighteousness. If we claim we have not
> sinned, we make him out to be a liar and his
> word is not in us. (1 John 1:8-10)
>
> My dear children, I write this to you so
> that you will not sin. But if anybody does sin,

---

[26] Matt 7:12   [27] Matt 7:2

we have an advocate with the Father—Jesus
Christ, the Righteous One. He is the atoning
sacrifice for our sins, and not only for ours
but also for the sins of the whole world. (1
John 2:1-2)

Now, it is inconceivable that anyone who sincerely
repents of their own sins and seeks forgiveness from God
would refuse to forgive others who have offended them.
The very idea of repentance implies forgiving those who
sin against us. We have no right to ask God to forget
our sins while we catalogue and dwell on the offences
committed against us. We have no right to expect God
to not condemn us while we condemn and seek revenge
against those who sin against us.

3.3.2   Vengeance is God's prerogative

The second reason why revenge is absolutely forbidden
in the New Covenant is that it is God's prerogative:
"vengeance is mine, says the Lord."[28] God has reserved
the right to exercise retribution as he sees fit, and does
not share this prerogative with anyone. Consequently,
the one who takes revenge against his neighbour usurps
the place of God, which is a sin against the Almighty.

In order to fully appreciate the requirement to not
take revenge, consider civilized human governments. The
right to exercise retribution is always vested in the ruling
authority, not the subject. Indeed, any attempt on the
part of the subject to exercise personal retribution and
take the law into their own hands is a criminal offence in
itself. The ruling authority establishes lawful means by

---

[28] Rom 12:19 NKJV

which the subject can seek justice, i.e. through the legal institutions and the courts.

Similar to human government, while God forbids personal vengeance under the divine administration, he has established the proper channels for seeking justice (discussed in the following sections). If we refuse to use the channels God has established and take matters into our own hands, we will be sinning against the divine Sovereign, and will be accountable to him.

3.4   Appealing to God for justice

Since God says "it is mine to avenge", instead of taking vengeance ourselves when we are wronged, we can appeal to God for retribution. As Solomon puts it: "Do not say, 'I'll pay you back for this wrong!' Wait for the LORD, and he will avenge you."[29]

Jesus taught the parable of the persistent widow to teach Christians that "they should always pray and not give up."[30] The widow appealed to the unjust judge, seeking justice and retribution against her adversaries. The judge, who neither feared God nor respected men, refused to consider the case of the widow. Yet, she was persistent and kept on coming to the judge for justice. In the end, the judge said to himself: "Even though I don't fear God or care what people think, yet because this widow keeps bothering me, I will see that she gets justice, so that she won't eventually come and attack me!"[31] The judge did not answer because he cared about God, justice or the woman. He answered because the woman was persistent in her request.

---

[29] Prov 20:22   [30] Luke 18:1-8   [31] Luke 18:4-5

Jesus contrasted the unjust judge with God. "Listen to what the unjust judge says. And will not God bring about justice for his chosen ones, who cry out to him day and night? Will he keep putting them off? I tell you, he will see that they get justice, and quickly."[32] First, unlike the unrighteous judge, God is just, and the justifier of those who appeal to him. Second, if an unrighteous judge will hear the case of a widow and stranger, how much more will God hear the prayer of his own elect and avenge them?

How can God say "it is mine to avenge, I will repay" and refuses to execute justice on behalf of his elect? How can he prohibit us from taking revenge ourselves and refuses to avenge us when we are wronged? Will God not execute justice for his elect who cry out day and night to him? Shall God not repay the wickedness committed against those who follow him? "He will avenge them speedily" is the promise of the Lord.

The main lesson from the foregoing discussion is that we should have absolute faith in God. When we are wronged, we should commit judgement to God, and wait for him.

The second lesson to remember is—like the persistent widow, we can pray to God for justice. Some Christians think praying for justice is contrary to the principle of grace and forgiveness. This is a mistake; justice is an essential part of forgiveness. There is a difference between justice and personal vengeance or revenge. Justice involves the concept of fairness, equitable retribution and rational consideration of the case. Revenge, on the other hand, is often an emotional and retaliatory action taken by an individual in response to wrongdoing. While jus-

---

[32] Luke 18:6-8

tice is impersonal and impartial, revenge is driven by personal interests and vindictiveness. Thus, while the New Testament absolutely prohibits us from taking personal revenge, seeking justice or redress for wrongdoing is perfectly in line with the principles of forgiveness and grace, as illustrated in the story of the widow.

What about prayers of vengeance, which are abundantly found in the Old Testament? Should Christians offer these kinds of imprecatory prayers? The Psalms especially are filled with the people of God praying for vengeance and invoking the wrath and curses of God upon their enemies. A notable example is Psalm 109, in which most of the verses call for vengeance against David's enemies. This is further discussed below.

Firstly, the wickedness of the enemy is established in the following verses:

> They attack me without cause ... repay me evil for good and hatred for my friendship ... never thought of doing a kindness ... but hounded to death the poor and the needy and the broken-hearted ... loved to pronounce a curse ... found no pleasure in blessing. (Psa 109:3,5,16,17)

David then goes on to curse the enemy and his family:

> Appoint someone evil to oppose my enemy; let an accuser stand at his right hand. When he is tried, let him be found guilty, and may his prayers condemn him. May his days be few; may another take his place of leadership. May his children be fatherless and his

wife a widow. May his children be wander-
ing beggars; may they be driven from their
ruined homes.

May a creditor seize all he has; may
strangers plunder the fruits of his labour.
May no one extend kindness to him or take
pity on his fatherless children. May his
descendants be cut off, their names blotted
out from the next generation. May the
iniquity of his fathers be remembered before
the LORD; may the sin of his mother never
be blotted out. May their sins always remain
before the LORD, that he may blot out their
name from the earth. (Psa 109:6-15)

The anger of David was not only triggered by the
wickedness committed against him, but also against the
helpless: the enemy "hounded to death the poor and
the needy and the brokenhearted."[33] This suggests that
David's concerns about the wicked was not only motivated by his personal interests, but by the welfare of the
helpless and the needy as well.

David invoked the wrath and curses of God against
the enemy, their wife, children, mother, father and descendants. This was in agreement with the Old Covenant
principle of God punishing future generations for the sins
of their ancestors. However, as discussed in Chapter 2,
this principle has been abolished by God in the fulfilment
of the New Covenant. The question is—are these prayers
of vengeance compliant with New Covenant principles of
grace, forgiveness and prohibition of personal vengeance?

An interesting passage on invoking the wrath of God

---

[33] Psa 109:16

against those who offend us can be found in Luke.

> Now it came to pass, when the time had
> come for Him to be received up, that He
> steadfastly set His face to go to Jerusalem,
> and sent messengers before His face. And
> as they went, they entered a village of the
> Samaritans, to prepare for Him. But they
> did not receive Him, because His face was
> set for the journey to Jerusalem. And when
> His disciples James and John saw this, they
> said, "Lord, do You want us to command
> fire to come down from heaven and consume
> them, just as Elijah did?" But He turned and
> rebuked them, and said, "You do not know
> what manner of spirit you are of. (Luke
> 9:51-55 NKJV)

The vengeful behaviour displayed by James and John
is quite astonishing. They felt so injured by the Samar-
itans' rejection of Christ that they thought calling down
fire from heaven to consume them would be justified.
Further, they considered such an act would be compliant
with Old Testament principles. Elijah called down the
fire of God to consume 153 solders[34] and the prophets
of Baal.[35] Elisha, his successor, also invoked the curse
of God on 42 children who mocked him and they were
instantly mulled to death by bears.[36]

Naturally, Christ rebuked the two disciples, remind-
ing them of the new principles of grace and forgiveness
he was establishing: "You do not know what manner of
spirit you are of." This should be a good reference point

---

[34] 2 Kings 10   [35] 1 Kings 18   [36] 2 Kings 2:23-24

for Christians regarding praying for vengeance against those who offend us. Christians should remember that the New Covenant has established a paradigm shift away from the old principles of vengeance.

Specifically, regarding praying for vengeance, the New Testament has the following to say:

> Bless those who curse you, pray for those who mistreat you. (Luke 6:28)

> Bless those who persecute you; bless and do not curse. (Rom 12:14)

> Do not repay evil with evil or insult with insult. On the contrary, repay evil with blessing, because to this you were called so that you may inherit a blessing. (1 Pet 3:9)

We are simply commanded to bless and not curse, by Christ, Paul and Peter. This means praying for vengeance is generally prohibited by the New Testament.

However, there is a context to the Scriptures above that should not be lost in interpretation. The command is to bless those who curse, insult or persecute "you" and not repay by cursing them back. In other words, the command prohibits cursing someone for personal revenge or from selfish motives. As discussed in Section 3.3, personal revenge in any form, including invoking curses in prayer, is prohibited in the New Testament. However, while invoking the wrath and curses of God on someone is prohibited in principle, there are situations in which this action is allowed for benevolent reasons. Indeed, in some circumstances, Christians may actually be under moral obligation to seek and invoke the wrath of God on some people.

For example, there may be circumstances where the wickedness of some people become so grave and insatiable to the extent that only a complete destruction by God would prevent further evil from being committed. In such cases, Christians must stand up to evil and invoke the wrath of God to annihilate those bent on atrocious acts.

Another example of invoking the vengeance of God for benevolent purposes is when dealing with people committed to perverting the Gospel of Christ. These are false prophets and teachers who know the truth of God, and yet obstinately propagate false doctrines to mislead people. Jesus himself was the first to curse such false prophets. And Paul also invoked the wrath and curse of God upon them.

> Woe to you, teachers of the law and Pharisees, you hypocrites! You shut the door of the kingdom of heaven in people's faces. You yourselves do not enter, nor will you let those enter who are trying to. (Matt 23:13)

> As we have already said, so now I say again: If anybody is preaching to you a gospel other than what you accepted, let them be under God's curse! (Gal 1:9)

> If anyone does not love the Lord, let that person be cursed! (1 Cor. 16:22)

The context of the last Scripture shows that the Apostle was not merely invoking curses on all unbelievers, but those who pretended to be believers among the

Corinthian Christians in order to lead them away from faith in Christ through false teaching.

The lesson here is that we should not be motivated by selfish interests or bruised ego when we pray for vengeance. Rather, we should seek the glory of God, the promotion of his interests and the highest well-being of others. This is the dividing line between personal revenge, which is prohibited by the New Testament, and invoking God's wrath and vengeance for benevolent purposes. The story of the two disciples rebuked by Christ shows that when one is zealous for the Gospel, one could still be driven by selfish motives. Thus, it is important to be grounded in the New Covenant principles of grace and forgiveness. We should also remember that "in the same way you judge others, you will be judged, and with the measure you use, it will be measured to you."[37]

Overall, Christians should be comfortable with appealing to God for justice when we are wronged and leaving the case with him, knowing that God will deal with it in his infinite wisdom. However, if our prayers mostly consist of requests for vengeance on others, then we need to reassess whether we ourselves are the ones who need forgiveness and healing.

3.5   Appealing to governing authorities

In addition to appealing directly to God for justice, we can also appeal to human government. The Scriptures

---

[37] Matt 7:2

describe governing authorities as servants of God, established to execute justice and retribution on his behalf.

> Let everyone be subject to the governing authorities, for there is no authority except that which God has established. The authorities that exist have been established by God. Consequently, whoever rebels against the authority is rebelling against what God has instituted, and those who do so will bring judgment on themselves. For rulers hold no terror for those who do right, but for those who do wrong.
>
> Do you want to be free from fear of the one in authority? Then do what is right and you will be commended. For the one in authority is God's servant for your good. But if you do wrong, be afraid, for rulers do not bear the sword for no reason. They are God's servants, agents of wrath to bring punishment on the wrongdoer. Therefore, it is necessary to submit to the authorities, not only because of possible punishment but also as a matter of conscience.
>
> This is also why you pay taxes, for the authorities are God's servants, who give their full time to governing. Give to everyone what you owe them: If you owe taxes, pay taxes; if revenue, then revenue; if respect, then respect; if honor, then honor. (Rom 13:1-7)

Paul makes two primary points in the above passage. First, governing authorities have been established by God, for there is no authority except that which God has established. Consequently, those who reject governmental authority reject God's authority. As a derived and limited authority, human government must be exercised for the well-being of its subjects. If not, they could be removed by God himself.[38]

Second, human governments, in accordance with God's purpose, execute justice and retribution on earth. In this capacity, those in authority are servants of God, agents of wrath to bring punishment on evil doers. While ultimate justice and vengeance belong to God, human governments have been appointed to hold the sword of God's vengeance against evil. They are sanctioned by God to execute equitable retribution. Thus, it is within the purpose of God for Christians to seek justice through the legal institutions established by human governments.

Elsewhere in Scripture, Paul also makes the following statements:

> If any of you has a dispute with another, do you dare to take it before the ungodly for judgment instead of before the Lord's people? Or do you not know that the Lord's people will judge the world? And if you are to judge the world, are you not competent to judge trivial cases? Do you not know that we will judge angels? How much more the things of this life!
>
> Therefore, if you have disputes about such matters, do you ask for a ruling from those whose way of life is scorned in the church? I say this to shame you. Is it possible that there is nobody among you wise enough to judge a

---

[38] Psa 75:7; Dan 2:21

dispute between believers? But instead, one brother takes another to court—and this in front of unbelievers!

The very fact that you have lawsuits among you means you have been completely defeated already. Why not rather be wronged? Why not rather be cheated? Instead, you yourselves cheat and do wrong, and you do this to your brothers and sisters. (1 Cor 6:1-8)

On the surface, the above passage from Paul seems to contradict his instructions regarding the governing authorities in Romans 13. However, the context of the Corinthian passage indicates he is dealing with a different issue in the Church, namely, the prevalence of lawsuits among members of the Church, and not the providential authority of human governments.

The Apostle observes that secular courts do not necessarily operate by Christian standards. Human governments are designed for the benefit of all the people, societies and cultures under their jurisdiction. These will include various religious and non-religious cultures and philosophies. Consequently, human governments are generally secular in nature and not expected to operate by Christian standards. While there may be common grounds among the moral frameworks of the various religious and non-religious systems, human governments must rise above the dividing lines in order to fulfil their mission. Consequently, they should not adopt the moral framework of any single religious or non-religious system.

More importantly, human governments can only generally regulate actual conduct, and have no capacity to regulate spiritual things. For example, the intention behind the conduct of a person is considered only to the extent that it can be demonstrated in the courts (e.g. as in a premeditated crime). Generally, while morality (religious or secular) is primarily concerned with the intention, purpose or willing, human governments are concerned with outward conduct. This is why sin, a religious concept, does not exist in civilized legal frameworks. Rather, the focus of human law is criminality of conduct or behaviour. Given the above distinction between Christian and governmental standards, Paul berates the Corinthian Church for rushing to courts without first following Scriptural principles.

Another point made by Paul is that increased lawsuits among Christians negatively impact the mission of Christ and the Church. Unlike human governments, the Churches of Christ are mandated to be witnesses and agents of the reconciliation of God.[39] Christians should not jeopardise this mission by going to court at first opportunity. Instead, they should follow the framework established by Christ himself for resolving disputes.

> If your brother or sister sins, go and point out their fault, just between the two of you. If they listen to you, you have won them over. But if they will not listen, take one or two others along, so that 'every matter may be established by the testimony of two or three witnesses.' If they still refuse to listen, tell it to the church; and if they refuse to listen even to the church, treat them as you would a pagan or a tax collector. (Matt 18:15-17)

---

[39] See Section 4.4

The Christian approach to resolving conflicts can be summarized as follows:

1. If possible, privately discuss the problem with the offender, and try to resolve the issue.

2. If private discussion is not possible or if the issue cannot be resolved, take one or two witnesses (i.e. a few people) with you to help mediate a solution.

3. If the issue still cannot be resolved, take the matter to the Church leadership.

4. If the Church cannot resolve the issue, the Christian may treat the offender as a pagan or a tax collector.[40] Treating the offender as a pagan or sinner means the Christian may sever relationship with the offender, if continuing relationship will be detrimental to the Christian or the mission of Christ.[41] Furthermore, the victim of the offence can also seek justice through the courts.

In all of the above steps, the assumption is that the offending party is the one who refuses to cooperate. It is assumed that the Christian has been reasonable and acted in good faith in their attempt to resolve the issue.

Paul berates the Corinthian Church for their readiness to file lawsuits against each other. His statements imply they did not follow the approach prescribed by Christ. Rather, they seemed to jump into lawsuits at first opportunity. Paul lamented the prevalence of lawsuits reported in the Church, suggesting this very fact

---

[40] At the time of Christ, tax collectors were seen as dishonest, traitors and grouped with sinners. [41] 2 Cor 6:14

meant they were already defeated. If the Church cannot resolve issues among members, how can they fulfil the mission of Christ as witnesses and agents of reconciliation in the world? How can the Church share in the glory of Christ when he comes back to judge the living and the dead at the appointed time?[42]

The foregoing discussion shows there is no contradiction between the two passages from Paul on Christians seeking justice through the courts. In summary, Christians are commanded to follow the framework established by Christ for resolving conflicts. In this framework, seeking justice through the courts is a last resort. However, if this becomes our first resort or if we frivolously file lawsuits against each other, then we ourselves might be the ones who need forgiveness and healing. Paul himself appealed to secular Roman laws on a number of occasions, when he found himself in the hands of violent enemies.[43]

---

[42] See Section 4.3.2   [43] Acts 16:37; 25:10

Chapter 4

Reconcile with the offender

The third step on the journey of forgiveness is reconciliation—a restoration of the previous relationship which has been destroyed by the offence. The forgiveness of God did not end with forgetting our past sins and not condemning us—he also reconciled us to himself. Through Christ, God restored the relationship and privileges that were lost through the sin of Adam. And he commissioned us to be agents of reconciliation in the world, making every effort to live in peace with all people, as far as it lies within our power.

In order to unravel the mystery of the reconciliation of mankind to God, one must understand the previous relationship man had with God prior to the Fall.

4.1 Prior to the Fall

The Scriptures provide glimpses into life prior to the Fall of man. In the Biblical creation narrative in Genesis, we are repeatedly told that everything God created was good: "God saw all that he had made, and it was very good."[1] If everything created was good, and all things were created by God,[2] then we can conclude that sin and evil entered the creation of God through the Fall. This is the central message presented in the account of the Fall of man in Genesis.

Man[3] was created in the image of God and was given dominion over all of God's creation.[4] As the ruler over God's creation, Adam was called "the son of God"[5] and enjoyed direct communion with God.[6] Adam's title as the son of God not only signified his direct creation by God, but also the intimacy he enjoyed with God before the Fall. Adam's relationship with God before the Fall parallels the relationship between Christ and the Father: while Adam was the son of God by creation, Christ was the Son of God by birth. Hence, Christ is also called "the last Adam."[7]

As the son of God, Adam was in a perfect union with God through the faculties of his spirit or mind. The light of the Holy Spirit reached Adam's spirit unimpeded, directing his mind and will, and ultimately his body. Peace and harmony reigned in the faculties of his mind, and in the garden of Eden, and over all of God's creation. Unfortunately, Adam disobeyed God, the Fall happened, and the peace and harmony was disrupted, plunging mankind

---

[1] Gen 1:31 [2] John 1:3 [3] Mankind or the human race, represented by Adam, the first human. [4] Gen 1:26-28 [5] Luke 3:38 [6] Gen 3:8 [7] 1 Cor 15:45

and the rest of creation into utter darkness.

4.2 Effects of the Fall

God commanded Adam regarding the fruit of the Tree of Knowledge of Good and Evil: "in the day that you eat of it you shall surely die."[8] Unfortunately, Adam and Eve disobeyed the command of God and ate of the fruit. Thus, in accordance with the word of God, they *died* on the same day they ate the fruit.[9]

To properly understand the kind of death experienced by Adam and Eve, we must define *death* in the Scriptures. The term death, as used in Scripture, means "a separation" of one entity from another.[10] The Scriptures distinguish between the following kinds of death:

- **Physical death** is the separation of the inner man (spirit and soul) from the body, "as the body without the spirit is dead."[11] When physical death occurs "the dust returns to the ground it came from, and the spirit returns to God who gave it."[12]

- **Spiritual death** is the separation of the inner man (spirit and soul) from God. Those who are spiritually dead are bodily alive but "dead in your transgressions and sins."[13] The Scripture says: "Your iniquities have separated you from your God; your

---

[8] Gen 2:17 NKJV   [9] Whether the Genesis narrative is literal or figurative is not our main concern here. Either way, the narrative establishes the doctrine of the Fall, which marks the transition of mankind from a state of obedience to a state of disobedience, sinfulness and darkness.   [10] See [dake] Notes on Eph 2:1,5   [11] James 2:26   [12] Eccl 12:7   [13] Eph 2:1; See also Col 2:13

sins have hidden his face from you, so that he will not hear."[14] Since God is the source of all light, spiritual death is the state of sinfulness. Jesus meant spiritual death when he told a prospective disciple: "Follow me, and let the dead bury their own dead."[15] People who are physically dead cannot bury dead bodies. Also, "the widow who lives for pleasure is dead even while she lives."[16] That is, she is spiritually dead while being physically alive.

- **Second death** is the second and eternal separation of man (body, spirit and soul) from God in the Lake of Fire. "But the cowardly, the unbelieving, the vile, the murderers, the sexually immoral, those who practice magic arts, the idolaters and all liars—they will be consigned to the fiery lake of burning sulfur. This is the second death."[17]

- **Death to sin** is the separation between man and sin.[18]

- **Death to the law** is the separation between the Christian and the Old Testament law.[19]

It is clear from the context of Genesis that Adam and Eve died spiritually on the same day they disobeyed the command of God. In other words, they were spiritually separated from God, the source of all light and revelation, and descended into a state of total sinfulness. This is the first and immediate effect of the Fall.

---

[14] Isa 59:2   [15] Matt 8:22   [16] 1 Tim 5:6   [17] Rev 21:8   [18] Rom 6:2,11; Heb 7:26   [19] Rom 7:4

4.2.1   Hostility between man and God

The effect of the Fall of man is summarised by the following Scripture:

> The mind governed by the flesh is hostile
> to God; it does not submit to God's law, nor
> can it do so. (Rom 8:7)

The word *hostility* means hatred, animosity, opposition, conflict, discord, etc. The Fall resulted in hostility between God and mankind, and consequently produced hostility within the nature of man. The wording of the Scripture indicates aggressive hostility towards God. The mind itself is the source and essence of the hostility towards God and his laws. In this fallen state, the human mind cannot, and will not, obey the law of God. Elsewhere, the Scriptures make this plain.

> But the natural man does not receive the
> things of the Spirit of God, for they are foolishness to him; nor can he know them, because they are spiritually discerned. (1 Cor
> 2:14 NKJV)

> No one can come to me unless the Father who sent me draws them, and I will raise
> them up at the last day. (John 6:44)

> As it is written: "There is no one righteous, not even one; there is no one who understands; there is no one who seeks God. All
> have turned away, they have together become
> worthless; there is no one who does good, not
> even one." (Rom 3:10-12)

> Remain in me, as I also remain in you. No branch can bear fruit by itself; it must remain in the vine. Neither can you bear fruit unless you remain in me. "I am the vine; you are the branches. If you remain in me and I in you, you will bear much fruit; apart from me you can do nothing. (John 15:4-5)

4.2.2 Hostility within man

Another consequence of the spiritual death of man is the corruption of the nature of man. As a result of the hostility between God and man, internally, the Fall also resulted in hostilities among the primary faculties of the mind. There are three primary faculties of the mind, namely, intellect, sensibility and will.[20] These are briefly described as follows:

- The **intellect** is the faculty that includes the reason, knowledge, understanding, conscience, self-consciousness. In particular, the conscience is the function that recognizes conformity or nonconformity of the heart and life to the moral law of God, pronouncing approval or disapproval in accordance with the requirements of the law.

- The **sensibility** is the faculty or susceptibility of feeling, sensation, desire, emotion, passion, pain, pleasure. The five senses (sight, hearing, taste, smell, and touch) belong to this faculty of the mind.

- The **will** is the executive faculty of man or the faculty of choosing, acting or doing. It is the faculty

---

[20] See [finney] p30

that chooses to obey or disobey the law of God, and thus is the proper object of command.

Prior to the Fall, these three faculties of the mind worked in perfect harmony, without any conflict or contention. The reason received light or knowledge through the Spirit of God, revealing moral obligation to love God and neighbour. The will executed the demands of the reason and conscience, in accordance with the moral law of God. The sensibilities, emotions and passions were subject to the law of God. The entire nature of man was in harmony with the nature of God, resulting in total submission to God and perfect obedience to the moral law.

Then the Fall happened, man died spiritually and the three faculties began to function in hostility against God and against each other. The pathway between the human mind and God, the source of light and moral obligation, was disrupted. Consequently, the mind no longer received light from the divine source, plunging mankind into spiritual darkness and sinfulness. The sensibilities, emotions and passions became corrupted, depraved and insatiable in their demands. Scripture describes the state of the fallen mind as follows:

> They are darkened in their understanding and separated from the life of God because of the ignorance that is in them due to the hardening of their hearts. Having lost all sensitivity, they have given themselves over to sensuality so as to indulge in every kind of impurity, and they are full of greed. (Eph 4:18-19)

The will became obstinate and committed to obeying the demands of the sensibilities and passions of the flesh, rather than the will of God revealed in the reason. From the moment of birth, the depraved sensibilities and passions act as a powerful impulse to the will, and secure its commitment to procure the gratification of the flesh. Over time, this commitment of the will to satisfying the demands of the flesh becomes a natural habit, hard to overcome. By the time the reason, conscience and the idea of moral obligation are gradually developed, the will has already formed the habit of seeking to fulfil the depraved demands of the sensibilities and passions. At this stage, the demands of the law of God are ignored by the will. Over time, the voice of God revealed within the reason and conscience becomes feeble and feeble.

In the worst cases, the nature of man became so depraved that the Scriptures describe people "whose consciences have been seared as with a hot iron."[21] That is, the consciences of these people have become so corrupted that they cannot morally distinguish between right and wrong. In extreme cases, such people even "exchanged the truth of God for the lie,"[22] incurring the wrath of God.

4.2.3 Hostility between man and neighbours

With hostility between man and God and within man himself, it is hardly surprising to see hostilities between man and his neighbours. If man cannot be at peace with God and within himself, then he cannot be at peace with

---

[21] 1 Tim 4:2   [22] Rom 1:25 NKJV

his neighbours. The history of mankind is tainted with hostilities and conflicts among various tribes, societies, nations and the rest of creation. Since records began, there has been constant hostilities among various levels of human organizations, with catastrophic consequences for both living and non-living things.

4.2.4 Secondary effects of the Fall

We have already discussed the primary effects of the Fall, namely, man lost the pure image of God, access to God, and was consequently plunged into spiritual death and darkness. In the following, we summarize the secondary effects of the Fall.

- **Diseases and physical death**. We have already seen that spiritual death was the primary fulfilment of the words of God: "for in the day that you eat of it you shall surely die."[23] Bodily infirmities, diseases and physical death were the secondary effects of the spiritual death experienced by man. In other words, the physical constitution of man began to die once Adam and Eve disobeyed God. "In the sweat of your face you shall eat bread till you return to the ground, for out of it you were taken; for dust you are, and to dust you shall return."[24]

  Through the toils of life, and within a cursed environment, the organs of the body are continually plagued by numerous diseases, as they age over time. Ultimately, the organs fail, leading to the death of the body. While it is unclear whether God

---

[23] Gen 2:17 NKJV   [24] Gen 3:19 NKJV

originally intended for man to somehow live physically forever, the Scriptures imply that the average lifespan of man was curtailed by the Fall.[25] The Scriptures admonish: "Remember your Creator in the days of your youth, before the days of trouble come ... before the silver cord is severed ... and the dust returns to the ground it came from, and the spirit returns to God who gave it."[26]

- **Loss of dominion**. Adam was created as the ruler of God's creation.[27] Following the Fall, man was cast out of the presence of God and lost his position as the ruler of God's creation. The Devil, who enticed Adam and Eve to sin, usurped the place of man and became the god and ruler of this world.[28]

- **Wrath and curses of God**. The Fall also brought the wrath and curses of God on mankind.[29] Eve was cursed with severe pains in childbirth and subordination to Adam. The environment was cursed for the sake of Adam—in sweat Adam would eat. The whole of creation was subjected to corruption, pending final restoration at the appointed time.[30] There were also curses for breaking the laws of God.[31]

4.3   Reconciled to God in Christ

Through Christ, God reconciled mankind back to himself, and restored the previous relationship that was lost

---

[25] Gen 6:3; Psa 90:10   [26] Eccl 12:1-7   [27] Gen 1:26-28   [28] 2 Cor 4:4; John 12:31; Eph 2:2   [29] Gen 3   [30] Rom 8:21-25   [31] Deut 28:15-20; Deut 27:26; Gal 3:10

through the sin of Adam. The following Scriptures summarize the reconciliation of God, through the atonement and ministry of Christ.

> For God was pleased to have all his fullness dwell in him, and through him to reconcile to himself all things, whether things on earth or things in heaven, by making peace through his blood, shed on the cross. Once you were alienated from God and were enemies in your minds because of your evil behavior. But now he has reconciled you by Christ's physical body through death to present you holy in his sight, without blemish and free from accusation. (Col 1:19-22)

> God was reconciling the world to himself in Christ, not counting people's sins against them. (2 Cor 5:19)

Christ made peace between mankind and God by destroying the hostilities that existed as a result of the Fall, giving man a new access to God.

> For he himself is our peace, who has made the two groups [Jew and Gentile] one and has destroyed the barrier, the dividing wall of hostility, by setting aside in his flesh the law with its commands and regulations. His purpose was to create in himself one new humanity out of the two, thus making peace, and in one body to reconcile both of them to God through the cross, by which he put to death their hostility. He came and preached

> peace to you who were far away and peace
> to those who were near. For through him we
> both have access to the Father by one Spirit.
> (Eph 2:14-18; See also Col 1:20)

Christ made peace through the pouring of his blood
on the cross, and restored the divine access lost by Adam.
He opened "a new and living way" for those who believe
in him, so that they can now approach the holiest presence of God without any impediment and with boldness.
Indeed, he himself is the way, the truth and the life—no
one can come to the Father without passing through him.
By virtue of his atonement, Christ is the one and only
mediator between God and mankind.

> Therefore, brothers and sisters, since we
> have confidence to enter the Most Holy Place
> by the blood of Jesus, by a new and living
> way opened for us through the curtain, that
> is, his body, ... let us draw near to God with
> a sincere heart. (Heb 10:19-22)

> Jesus answered, "I am the way and the
> truth and the life. No one comes to the Father
> except through me." (John 14:6)

> Nor is there salvation in any other, for
> there is no other name under heaven given
> among men by which we must be saved. (Acts
> 4:12 NKJV)

The Scriptures recognise the parallel between Adam's
disobedience and Christ's obedience, and the impact
of both on mankind. Christ himself is called "the last

Adam"[32] who came to repair the damage caused by the first Adam. Whereas the first Adam disobeyed and brought damnation upon mankind, the last Adam obeyed and brought blessings.[33]

The reconciliation of Christ not only restored man's access to God, but also the key privileges lost through the Fall were restored, as summarized in the following subsections.

4.3.1 Restoration of the image of God

As already mentioned in Section 4.1, Adam was created in the image or likeness of God. This primarily deals with spiritual and moral likeness to God, typically termed communicable attributes of God. These are the attributes God shares with humans in some form. Examples of our spiritual likeness to God are reason, understanding, conscience, will, etc. Examples of our moral likeness to God are love, grace, mercy, goodness, etc.

In Section 4.2, we saw how the Fall introduced hostilities between God and man, and within the primary faculties of the mind; impeding the harmony that existed among them since creation. By restoring man's access to God, Christ opened a pathway for the light of God to reach man's faculties, thereby restoring the harmony and the pure image of God. More importantly, the atonement and salvation allowed the Holy Spirit of God to dwell in the temple of the inner man, so he can form the image of God in us.

Because you are his sons, God sent the

---

[32] 1 Cor 15:45 [33] See Romans 5 for extended discussion by apostle Paul

> Spirit of his Son into our hearts, the Spirit who calls out, "Abba, Father." (Gal 4:6)

> Do you not know that your bodies are temples of the Holy Spirit, who is in you, whom you have received from God? You are not your own; you were bought at a price. Therefore honor God with your bodies. (1 Cor 6:19-20; See also 2 Cor 6:16)

The dwelling of the Holy Spirit in the inner man is one of the central doctrines of the Christian Faith. The primary purpose of the indwelling Holy Spirit is to produce fruit consistent with the moral and spiritual nature of God; and thereby restore the image of God corrupted by the Fall.

> But the fruit of the Spirit is love, joy, peace, forbearance, kindness, goodness, faithfulness, gentleness and self-control. Against such things there is no law. (Gal 5:22-23)

Secondly, the indwelling Holy Spirit is God's seal of ownership and authority over the Christian, and is a guarantee of their inheritance until the final redemption.

> When you believed, you were marked in him with a seal, the promised Holy Spirit, who is a deposit guaranteeing our inheritance until the redemption of those who are God's possession—to the praise of his glory. (Eph 1:13-14)

Thirdly, the indwelling Holy Spirit makes intercession for us in accordance with the will of God.[34]

---

[34] See Section 6.1.2

In the same way, the Spirit helps us in our weakness. We do not know what we ought to pray for, but the Spirit himself intercedes for us through wordless groans. (Rom 8:26)

For who knows a person's thoughts except their own spirit within them? In the same way no one knows the thoughts of God except the Spirit of God. (1 Cor 2:11)

Finally, the indwelling Holy Spirit operates his gifts through us, for the broader purpose of building the Church of Christ (discussed in Section 5.1.2).

4.3.2 Restoration of man's dominion

The atonement of Christ also restored the dominion lost by Adam to the Devil.[35] Christ acquired all authority in heaven and on earth[36] and has passed this authority on to those who believe in him.

All authority in heaven and on earth has been given to me. (Matt 28:18)

I have given you authority to trample on snakes and scorpions and to overcome all the power of the enemy; nothing will harm you. (Luke 10:19)

Or do you not know that the Lord's people will judge the world? And if you are to judge the world, are you not competent to judge

---

[35] See Section 4.2.4   [36] See Section 6.1.1

trivial cases? Do you not know that we will judge angels? How much more the things of this life! (1 Cor 6:2-3)

As the above Scriptures show, the dominion lost by man through the Fall has been restored by Christ, who raised man to his rightful place. Indeed, Christ exalted man above his original place in the hierarchy of authority. Originally, man was created "a little lower than the angels."[37] Following the atonement and subsequent salvation, man has been adopted as a son and made co-heir with Christ.

Now if we are children, then we are heirs—heirs of God and co-heirs with Christ, if indeed we share in his sufferings in order that we may also share in his glory. (Rom 8:17)

As co-heirs with Christ, Christians share in his glory and authority. For example, just as the Devil and his demons are subject to Christ, so are they subject to those who have been adopted as sons of God. Just as Christ by his atonement became the Judge of the living and the dead,[38] so will Christians judge the world and angels. The authority of the redeemed will be complete when they shall rule over all of God's creation with Christ upon his return.[39]

4.3.3 Removal of the curses

As discussed in Section 4.2.4, the Fall also resulted in the wrath and curses of God. These included curses on child-

---

[37] Heb 2:7; Psa 8:5   [38] See Section 6.1.1   [39] Rev 5:10; 20:4-6; Gal 3:29; 2 Tim 2:12

birth and the environment, as well as curses for breaking the laws of God. As part of his atonement, "Christ redeemed us from the curse of the law by becoming a curse for us."[40] This means, instead of incurring the wrath and curses of God when we fall short, we rather obtain mercy when we confess our sins and repent from them.

While Christ dealt with the curses of the law, some curses still remain pending the final redemption of all creation. For example, the severity of pains in childbirth still remains. However, God has promised salvation: "But women will be saved through childbearing—if they continue in faith, love and holiness with propriety"[41]

In the final restoration of all things, God has assured us that all curses will be removed: "No longer will there be any curse."[42] For further details on the final restoration of all things, see Section 4.5.

4.4   Ministry of reconciliation

The Scriptures state that following his own mission of reconciling the world to himself, God committed to Christians the ministry of reconciliation.

> All this is from God, who reconciled us to himself through Christ and gave us the ministry of reconciliation: that God was reconciling the world to himself in Christ, not counting people's sins against them. And he has committed to us the message of reconciliation. We are therefore Christ's ambassadors, as though God were making his ap-

---

[40] Gal 3:13   [41] 1 Tim 2:15   [42] Rev 22:3

peal through us. We implore you on Christ's behalf: Be reconciled to God. (2 Cor 5:18-20)

The purpose of God in committing to Christians the ministry of reconciliation is to help him achieve the final restoration of all creation. There are two parts of this ministry. Firstly, the ministry primarily deals with spreading the Gospel of Christ. That is, God through Christ has reconciled mankind to himself, and that all who believe in Christ will be reconciled to God. In this first part of the ministry, Christians are witnesses to the Gospel and Christ's ambassadors, and have been sent to the world to share the good news.

Go into all the world and preach the gospel to all creation. (Mark 16:15)

But you will receive power when the Holy Spirit comes on you; and you will be my witnesses in Jerusalem, and in all Judea and Samaria, and to the ends of the earth. (Acts 1:8)

The second part of the ministry of reconciliation is that, in his grand scheme, God will ultimately reconcile the whole of creation to himself. This will complete the final restoration of the damage caused by the Fall of mankind and angels.[43] This process began with himself in the atonement of Christ, and will continue until the restoration of all creation is complete. In this plan, God has commanded Christians to be not only witnesses, but actual agents of reconciliation in the world. Consequently, they are expected to act in every situation to

---

[43] Acts 3:20-21; Rom 8:21-22

bring about reconciliation whenever possible. Reconciliation is so central to the mission of Christ that we are told to suspend our own service to God till we have first reconciled with those who offend us.

> Therefore, if you are offering your gift at the altar and there remember that your brother or sister has something against you, leave your gift there in front of the altar. First go and be reconciled to them; then come and offer your gift. (Matt 5:23-24)

The clear implication of the above Scripture is that our service will not be accepted unless we have exhausted all efforts on our part to reconcile with those who offend us. If we refuse to reconcile with others, we cannot be effective witnesses to the reconciliation of God. "Blessed are the peacemakers, for they will be called children of God."[44]

4.5 Reconciliation not always possible

While reconciliation is an important part of forgiveness, sometimes, it is simply not possible to achieve a full restoration of the previous relationship. For various reasons, reconciliation may be complete, partial or simply impossible. The Scriptures recognise this fact and provide the framework for Christians to follow in such cases.

> If your brother or sister sins, go and point out their fault, just between the two of you. If

---

[44] Matt 5:9

they listen to you, you have won them over. But if they will not listen, take one or two others along, so that 'every matter may be established by the testimony of two or three witnesses.' If they still refuse to listen, tell it to the church; and if they refuse to listen even to the church, treat them as you would a pagan or a tax collector. (Matt 18:15-17)

If it is possible, as far as it depends on you, live at peace with everyone. (Rom 12:18)

Make every effort to live in peace with everyone and to be holy. (Heb 12:14)

Several principles are specified in the Scriptures above. Firstly, there is an implicit acknowledgement that reconciliation is not always possible. Christ himself prescribed the steps Christians should follow in resolving conflict and pursuing reconciliation with their neighbours (discussed in Section 3.5). He acknowledged that after pursuing all the steps mentioned, reconciliation may still not be possible.

Secondly, the Christian is under moral obligation to do everything in their power to bring about reconciliation. The limit of this obligation is defined by the phrase "as far as it depends on you," reconcile with the offender. That is, the Christian is expected to make every effort towards reconciliation. It is also important to note that there is no time limit to this obligation: the Christian should be prepared to reconcile whenever it is possible. That is, if the circumstances change in the future and reconciliation becomes possible, the Christian should embrace the opportunity to reconcile. Jesus emphasised this principle when he told Peter to be prepared to forgive "up to seventy times seven,"[45] effectively unlimited times.

Thirdly, when reconciliation is ultimately impossible after exhausting all reasonable efforts, this outcome does not diminish the forgiveness and is accepted by God. The Christian in such cases should not be impacted by any guilt on the failure to achieve a full restoration. In the words of Christ, if all reasonable efforts towards reconciliation fail, the Christian may treat the offender as a pagan. In other words, the Christian is allowed to end fellowship with them if continual fellowship will be detrimental to the Christian or their mission.

> Do not be yoked together with unbelievers. For what do righteousness and wickedness have in common? Or what fellowship can light have with darkness? What harmony is there between Christ and Belial? Or what does a believer have in common with an unbeliever? (2 Cor 6:14-15)

However, as already remarked, if the circumstances change and reconciliation become possible in the future, the Christian should embrace the opportunity.

In the following subsections, we discuss various scenarios of full and partial reconciliation, as well as cases when reconciliation was actually not possible.

4.5.1 Partial reconciliation: God and creation

We have already seen in Section 4.3 how God reconciled sinful mankind to himself through the atonement

---

[45] Matt 18:21-22 NKJV

and intercession of Christ. Peace between God and man was achieved by Christ destroying the hostilities which the Fall of man created. However, the reconciliation of mankind and creation to God is only partial at this stage, pending a full restoration of all things at the appointed time. The following Scriptures make this plain.

> Jesus Christ, who was preached to you before, whom heaven must receive until the times of restoration of all things, which God has spoken by the mouth of all His holy prophets since the world began. (Acts 3:20-21 NKJV)

> For the creation was subjected to frustration, not by its own choice, but by the will of the one who subjected it, in hope that the creation itself will be liberated from its bondage to decay and brought into the freedom and glory of the children of God. We know that the whole creation has been groaning as in the pains of childbirth right up to the present time. Not only so, but we ourselves, who have the firstfruits of the Spirit, groan inwardly as we wait eagerly for our adoption to sonship, the redemption of our bodies. For in this hope we were saved. (Rom 8:20-24)

The final and full reconciliation of the children of God and the rest of creation awaits the second coming of Christ. Thus, even in the plan of salvation by God, a full reconciliation has to wait till the time when it shall be possible.

4.5.2 Impossible reconciliation: Unbelievers

When we talk of the reconciliation of mankind to God, it easy to forget that there are people for whom this reconciliation is impossible. As we saw in Section 3.3.1, God's plan of forgiveness and salvation is conditioned upon repentance and faith in Christ and his redemptive sacrifice. This implies anyone unwilling to fulfil the above conditions cannot be saved by the atonement of Christ. The Scriptures makes it abundantly clear that not all people shall be saved and reconciled to God.[46] In the final scheme of all things, those who accept Christ and are reconciled will spend eternity with God in heaven while those who refuse Christ will be separated and spend eternity in hell.[47] Thus, in God's plan of salvation, reconciliation of unrepentant and unbelieving people is impossible. Nonetheless, God accepts this impossibility, and is happy to be able to save those who commit themselves to Christ for salvation.

4.5.3 Full reconciliation: Paul and John Mark

Another example of reconciliation is the case of Paul, Barnabas and John Mark. While Paul and Barnabas prepared to embark on their second missionary journey, a disagreement arose between them regarding whether John Mark should accompany them.

Some time later Paul said to Barnabas,

---

[46] Rev 21:8; Matt 25:31-45; 7:13-23; Luke 13:23-25; Mark 4:15-17; James 4:4; 1 John 3:8-10   [47] John 5:28-29

"Let us go back and visit the believers in all
the towns where we preached the word of the
Lord and see how they are doing." Barnabas
wanted to take John, also called Mark, with
them, but Paul did not think it wise to take
him, because he had deserted them in Pam-
phylia and had not continued with them in
the work. They had such a sharp disagreement that they parted company. Barnabas
took Mark and sailed for Cyprus, but Paul
chose Silas and left, commended by the believers to the grace of the Lord. (Acts 15:36-
40)

The controversy over John Mark was no simple disagreement. While Barnabas wanted to take John Mark
along, Paul thought they should not take someone who
previously abandoned them on the first missionary journey. The disagreement was so severe Paul and Barnabas
separated, with each going on their own missionary journey.

There has been a considerable debate among Christians regarding who was right in this controversy over
Mark. Ignoring the details of the disagreement, the biblical evidence is that, ultimately, Paul and John Mark
reconciled, and worked together for the purpose of the
Gospel. We know that Mark worked closely with Paul
during the imprisonment of the latter in Rome,[48] and
Paul developed respect and love for Mark.[49] In his second epistle to Timothy, Paul writes: "Get Mark and bring
him with you, because he is helpful to me in my ministry."[50] What a change in Paul and Mark, and what a

---

[48] Phil 1:23   [49] Col 4:10   [50] 2 Tim 4:11

beautiful story of reconciliation!

4.5.4 Full reconciliation: Joseph and brothers

The story of Joseph and his brothers is quite a remarkable illustration of the journey of forgiveness and reconciliation.[51] Joseph was sold into slavery by his brothers out of jealousy. Through Joseph's humble character and the providence of God, the fortunes of Joseph dramatically turned around for the better, and he became the governor of Egypt, second only to the Pharaoh. When his brothers unknowingly came to bow before him, to seek refuge from severe famine, Joseph initially hid his identity from them. Joseph put his brothers to the test by treating them harshly to see if they had changed their behaviour. Initially, the brothers never asked for forgiveness from Joseph. However, at the time of the death of Jacob, their father, the brothers asked for forgiveness through their father. Recognising the divine purpose in all of his struggles, Joseph gladly forgave his brothers and assured them. This was a long journey of forgiveness and reconciliation, guided by the divine hand.

When Joseph's brothers saw that their father was dead, they said, "What if Joseph holds a grudge against us and pays us back for all the wrongs we did to him?" So they sent word to Joseph, saying, "Your father left these instructions before he died: 'This is what you are to say to Joseph: I ask you to forgive your

---

[51] Gen 37-50

brothers the sins and the wrongs they committed in treating you so badly.' Now please forgive the sins of the servants of the God of your father." When their message came to him, Joseph wept.

His brothers then came and threw themselves down before him. "We are your slaves," they said. But Joseph said to them, "Don't be afraid. Am I in the place of God? You intended to harm me, but God intended it for good to accomplish what is now being done, the saving of many lives. So then, don't be afraid. I will provide for you and your children." And he reassured them and spoke kindly to them. (Gen 50:15-21)

Chapter 5

Do good to the offender

The fourth step on the journey of forgiveness consists in doing good to those who hate and harm us. As usual, this concept is rooted in God's own action in forgiving us: he forgot our past sins, did not condemn us, reconciled us to himself, and blessed us with goodness. We will explore how God, in forgiving us, demonstrated his goodness towards us, and how he expects us to exercise the same towards those who offend us.

5.1   Goodness of God towards us

The Scriptures state that after forgiving and reconciling believers in Christ, God "blessed us in the heavenly realms with every spiritual blessing in Christ."[1] Firstly, these blessings are spiritual, in the sense that they primarily deal with the spirit and soul of man. Secondly, the blessings include not only the privileges lost by Adam through the Fall, but also new blessings that have been

---
[1] Eph 1:3

made possible through the ministry of Christ. Furthermore, the blessings that came through Christ also include physical blessings regarding the welfare of the body.

The primary demonstration of the love and goodness of God towards believers is revealed in the atonement of Christ. In our sinful, rebellious state, while the human mind was hostile towards God and his moral law, Christ died and reconciled us to God.[2] In Section 4.3, we discussed how through the atonement, the blessings lost by Adam in the Fall have been restored by Christ. These included restoration of the image of God, man's access to God, dominion over God's creation, as well as cancellation of the curses brought by the Fall. In the sections that follow, we will summarize additional key blessings that have been afforded to Christians through the ministry of Christ.

5.1.1   Unlimited forgiveness

A key blessing that has been made possible by the atonement of Christ is unlimited forgiveness of future sins by God. Not only did God cancel the original death penalty and curses brought by the Fall, he also made provision to forgive all of the future sins of those who have committed themselves to Christ for salvation.

There are two things which the Scriptures regard as absolutely indispensable conditions of salvation—that is, without them, no one can be saved. These are faith and holiness, as described in the following passages:

> Without faith it is impossible to please God. (Heb 11:6)

---

[2] Rom 5:8

> Without holiness no one will see the Lord.
> (Heb 12:14)

Faith and holiness are so interwoven and spread out in the Scriptures (particularly the New Testament), that even the casual reader cannot escape them. The relationship between the two is that of cause and effect: faith is the cause, holiness or obedience to Jesus is the effect. In other words, sincere and genuine faith must always lead to holy living for Christ.

The holiness that God requires is a sincere, genuine and willing commitment of the body, soul and spirit in obedience to Christ. Jesus summarized it as follows: "love the Lord your God with all your heart, with all your soul, and with all your mind" and "love your neighbor as yourself."[3] That is, whatever is your strength, dedicate it to loving God supremely and your neighbour as yourself. Notice the apostle does not say without a sinless state no one will see the Lord. As long as we live on Earth, no Christian will ever attain a sinless state, i.e. a state of total freedom from sin, moral fault or weakness. Indeed, God knows Christians may occasionally fall into sin and has made provision to forgive their future sins conditional on repentance.

> If we claim to be without sin, we deceive ourselves and the truth is not in us. If we confess our sins, he is faithful and just and will forgive us our sins and purify us from all unrighteousness. If we claim we have not sinned, we make him out to be a liar and his word is not in us. (1 John 1:8-10)

---

[3] Matt 22:37-40

> My dear children, I write this to you so
> that you will not sin. But if anybody does sin,
> we have an advocate with the Father—Jesus
> Christ, the Righteous One. He is the atoning
> sacrifice for our sins, and not only for ours
> but also for the sins of the whole world. (1
> John 2:1-2)

Note that forgiveness of future sins is not automatic:
future sins must be confessed and repented of, once
they are brought to knowledge by the Holy Spirit,
before they can be forgiven! Thus, Paul can say to
Christians: "Godly sorrow brings repentance that leads
to salvation."[4]

5.1.2   Gifts of the Holy Spirit

The gifts of the Holy Spirit represent another key blessing bestowed on Christians by God. In Section 4.3.1,
we discussed how the moral and spiritual image of God
was restored through the indwelling presence of the Holy
Spirit. The Holy Spirit accomplishes this task of form-
ing God's image through the fruits he bears in our lives.
Furthermore, the Holy Spirit operates his gifts through us
for the broader purpose of building the Church of Christ.
The gifts of the Holy Spirit are supernatural graces which
God has bestowed on individual Christians for the purpose of edifying, exhorting and comforting the Church
of Christ. The gifts are diverse, each with its own function towards building and demonstrating God's goodness
towards his Church.

---

[4] 2 Cor 7:10

We have different gifts, according to the grace given to each of us. If your gift is prophesying, then prophesy in accordance with your faith; if it is serving, then serve; if it is teaching, then teach; if it is to encourage, then give encouragement; if it is giving, then give generously; if it is to lead, do it diligently; if it is to show mercy, do it cheerfully. (Rom 12:6-8)

To one there is given through the Spirit a message of wisdom, to another a message of knowledge by means of the same Spirit, to another faith by the same Spirit, to another gifts of healing by that one Spirit, to another miraculous powers, to another prophecy, to another distinguishing between spirits, to another speaking in different kinds of tongues, and to still another the interpretation of tongues. (1 Cor 12:8-10)

And God has placed in the church first of all apostles, second prophets, third teachers, then miracles, then gifts of healing, of helping, of guidance, and of different kinds of tongues. (1 Cor 12:28)

5.1.3 Healing of sicknesses

As discussed in Section 4.2.4, diseases and bodily infirmities are consequences of the Fall of man. The Scriptures state that healing from diseases and infirmities of the body is one of the physical blessings brought by the atonement of Christ. Isaiah foresaw this blessing of physical healing via the atonement and proclaimed: "by his wounds we are healed."[5] Thus, in the fulfilment of the New Covenant, God specifically made provisions for the healing of diseases and infirmities of the body, as confirmed by the Scriptures below.

> "He himself bore our sins" in his body on the cross, so that we might die to sins and live for righteousness; "by his wounds you have been healed." (1 Pet 2:24)

> Is anyone among you sick? Let them call the elders of the church to pray over them and anoint them with oil in the name of the Lord. And the prayer offered in faith will make the sick person well; the Lord will raise them up. If they have sinned, they will be forgiven. Therefore confess your sins to each other and pray for each other so that you may be healed. The prayer of a righteous person is powerful and effective. (James 5:14-16)

Christ himself empathized the importance of physical healing in his own ministry on Earth by making it a central objective.

> Jesus went through all the towns and villages, teaching in their synagogues, proclaiming the good news of the kingdom and healing every disease and sickness. (Matt 9:35)

> How God anointed Jesus of Nazareth with the Holy Spirit and power, and how he went

---

[5] Isa 53:5

around doing good and healing all who were under the power of the devil, because God was with him. (Acts 10:38)

Heal the sick, raise the dead, cleanse those who have leprosy, drive out demons. Freely you have received; freely give. (Matt 10:7-8)

5.2 Doing good to the offender

Just as God demonstrated his goodness to us while we were still his enemies, we are commanded to demonstrate the same goodness towards those who offend us.

But to you who are listening I say: Love your enemies, do good to those who hate you, bless those who curse you, pray for those who mistreat you .... Do to others as you would have them do to you. If you love those who love you, what credit is that to you? Even sinners love those who love them. And if you do good to those who are good to you, what credit is that to you? Even sinners do that. And if you lend to those from whom you expect repayment, what credit is that to you? Even sinners lend to sinners, expecting to be repaid in full.

But love your enemies, do good to them, and lend to them without expecting to get anything back. Then your reward will be great, and you will be children of the Most High, because he is kind to the ungrateful and wicked. Be merciful, just as your Father is merciful. (Luke 6:26-36; See also Matt 5:43-48)

Bless those who persecute you; bless and do not curse .... If your enemy is hungry, feed him; if he is thirsty, give him something to drink. In doing this, you will heap burning coals on his head. Do not be overcome by evil, but overcome evil with good. (Rom 12:14-21)

Do not repay evil with evil or insult with insult. On the contrary, repay evil with blessing, because to this you were called so that you may inherit a blessing. (1 Pet 3:9)

Several principles are stated in the above Scriptures. Firstly, we are commanded to love our enemies. There is only one kind of love that can be a proper object of command. This is *agape love* or disinterested benevolence[6]—willing and seeking the highest good or well-being of others without selfish motives. This is the kind of love demonstrated by God towards us, which he expects us to exercise towards others, including those who offend us.[7]

Secondly, we are commanded to do good to those who hate and offend us. By doing so, we will overcome evil with good and "heap burning coals on their head." In other words, when we do good to those who offend us, we are unloading burning shame on them, which could ultimately result in their repentance and reconciliation.

---

[6] See "Attributes of Love" in [finney]   [7] John 3:16; Matt 22:37; 1 Cor 13; Matt 22:37-40; Gal 5:14; Rom 13:8-10; James 2:8

We are commanded to be like God, who "causes his sun to rise on the evil and the good, and sends rain on the righteous and the unrighteous."[8]

Thirdly, we are commanded to pray for our enemies—a task which has been covered in Chapter 6.

Finally, just as God forgives us when we confess our sins,[9] so are we required to forgive our neighbours, even "up to seventy times seven,"[10] i.e. unlimited times.

God expects Christians to follow his example in doing good to those who offend them. Admittedly, this is not an easy task. However, the instructions of God are clear and emphatic. The overall message of Scripture is: Christians must overcome evil with good, and thereby help advance the ultimate objective of God on earth, which is the full restoration of all creation to himself.

---

[8] Matt 5:45   [9] John 1:8-10   [10] Matt 18:21-22 NKJV

Chapter 6

Pray for the offender

The final step on the journey of forgiveness is to pray for the offender. This is the ultimate and most glorious step in following God on his journey from unforgiveness to absolute forgiveness. God has already taken this step for us in the mission of Christ, and he expects us to extend the same favour towards those who offend us. As usual, we will first review the example of God, and apply the lessons to explain his instructions to us.

6.1   Christ our intercessor

The forgiveness journey of God did not end with the atonement of Christ. The Scriptures state that, following his death and resurrection, Christ sat at the right-hand of God, continually making intersession for us.

> Who then is the one who condemns? No one. Christ Jesus who died—more than that, who was raised to life—is at the right hand

of God and is also interceding for us. (Rom 8:34)

My dear children, I write this to you so that you will not sin. But if anybody does sin, we have an advocate with the Father—Jesus Christ, the Righteous One. (1 John 2:1)

For there is one God and one mediator between God and mankind, the man Christ Jesus. (1 Tim 2:5)

Christ is described as our mediator and advocate, seated at the right-hand of God, making intersection for us. In order to unravel the purpose of the advocacy and intercession of Christ, one needs to properly understand the divine court system. Similar to human judicial court systems, the Scriptures describe the divine court as an arrangement in which there is a judge (God the Father), an advocate (Christ) and an accuser (Satan). The role of the advocate parallels that of the accuser: while the advocate pleads our cause in the divine court, the accuser brings charges against us. The role of Satan as the accuser in the divine court is described in the Scriptures as follows:

Then I heard a loud voice in heaven say: "Now have come the salvation and the power and the kingdom of our God, and the authority of his Messiah. For the accuser of our brothers and sisters, who accuses them before our God day and night, has been hurled down. (Rev 12:10)

Then he showed me Joshua the high priest standing before the angel of the LORD, and Satan standing at his right side to accuse him. The LORD said to Satan, "The LORD rebuke you, Satan! The LORD, who has chosen Jerusalem, rebuke you! Is not this man a burning stick snatched from the fire?" Now Joshua was dressed in filthy clothes as he stood before the angel. The angel said to those who were standing before him, "Take off his filthy clothes." Then he said to Joshua, "See, I have taken away your sin, and I will put fine garments on you." (Zech 3:1-4)

In the above Scriptures, Satan is described as the accuser of our brothers and sisters, who accuses them day and night before God. Christians are admonished to be vigilant of this adversary so they do not give him the opportunity to submit accusations against them in the court of heaven.[1] The story of Job is a good illustration of the tactics used by the accuser against the children of God.[2] While Job is described by God as "blameless and upright, a man who fears God and shuns evil,"[3] the accuser counteracts the testimony of God by charging Job with selfish motive in his piety. The accuser then challenges God to allow Job to be tested. The omniscience of God could not protect Job from been tested. Indeed, the natural attributes of God (such as omnipotence, omniscience, etc.) do not protect anyone without the legal foundation acquired via Christ's atonement.

---

[1] 1 Pet 5:8   [2] Job 1:6-12, 2:1-8   [3] Job 1:8

Christ's advocacy and intercession is an integral part of the atonement plan of God. In his suffering, Job lamented the lack of a mediator: "If only there were someone to mediate between us, someone to bring us together."[4] Prior to the atonement, Christ had not solidified his legal position as the mediator and advocate of mankind. Consequently, the defence of the accused in the divine court was limited and only relied on the general fairness and justice of God. Thus, one of the key reasons for the atonement was to furnish Christ with the legal foundation to be able to defend those who appeal to him. This is what makes Christ's intercession effective, further discussed in the following subsections.

6.1.1 Seated at the right hand of God

A key reason why Christ's intercession is effective is that he acquired the legal authority to mediate between God and mankind. The Scriptures describe Christ as sitting on the "right-hand of God", which symbolizes the power he legally acquired through his atonement. That is, by virtue of his atonement, all power has been legally vested in him, meaning he is able to save and defend all who call upon him, notwithstanding the constant accusations of the Devil. In his own words after the resurrection, Christ said: "All authority in heaven and on earth has been given to me."[5] Furthermore, the Scriptures describe his atonement and subsequent exaltation as follows:

> Christ Jesus: who, being in very nature God, did not consider equality with God something to be used to his own advantage;

---

[4] Job 9:33   [5] Matt 28:18

> rather, he made himself nothing by taking the very nature of a servant, being made in human likeness. And being found in appearance as a man, he humbled himself by becoming obedient to death—even death on a cross! Therefore God exalted him to the highest place and gave him the name that is above every name, that at the name of Jesus every knee should bow, in heaven and on earth and under the earth, and every tongue acknowledge that Jesus Christ is Lord, to the glory of God the Father. (Phil 2:5-11)

The power acquired by Christ through the atonement is not the same power he has always possessed by virtue of his divinity.

Firstly, through the atonement, Christ acquired the *power of attorney*, which allows him to act in the place of those who appeal to him. That means, he is able to pass the benefits of his atonement and righteousness to them.

> Therefore he is able to save completely those who come to God through him, because he always lives to intercede for them. (Heb 7:25)

Secondly, through his incarnation Christ became "the last Adam."[6] By learning obedience as the Son of God, through the suffering of the atonement, he became the rightful heir of God, reclaiming back the inheritance lost by the first Adam in the Fall.

---

[6] 1 Cor 15:45; Heb 1:5

> In these last days he [God] has spoken to
> us by his Son, whom he appointed heir of all
> things, and through whom also he made the
> universe. (Heb 1:2)

> Son though he was, he learned obedience
> from what he suffered and, once made perfect,
> he became the source of eternal salvation for
> all who obey him (Heb 5:8-9)

Thirdly, by virtue of his atonement, Christ was made
the Lord of all creation.[7] His name, which is his identity,
has been exalted above every other name in the entire
Universe to the end that everyone must acknowledge his
lordship. As Lord of all creation, he is also the Judge
of all of mankind, who will answer to him at the day of
judgement. That is, the one who suffered and died for our
sins will be the same who will judge us. In this capacity,
Christ has the power to pronounce reward or punishment
to every human being in accordance with their response
to the Gospel.

> Moreover, the Father judges no one, but
> has entrusted all judgment to the Son, that
> all may honor the Son just as they honor the
> Father. (John 5:22-23)

> For we must all appear before the judg-
> ment seat of Christ, so that each of us may re-
> ceive what is due us for the things done while
> in the body, whether good or bad. (2 Cor
> 5:10)

---

[7] Phil 2:5-11

> He [Christ] commanded us to preach to the people and to testify that he is the one whom God appointed as judge of the living and the dead. (Acts 10:42)

> For he [God] has set a day when he will judge the world with justice by the man he has appointed. He has given proof of this to everyone by raising him from the dead. (Acts 17:31)

6.1.2 He understands our infirmities

Another reason why Christ's intercession is effective is that, by virtue of having taken on human form, he understands our needs and infirmities. The Scriptures make this clear, as in the following:

> For we do not have a high priest who is unable to empathize with our weaknesses, but we have one who has been tempted in every way, just as we are—yet he did not sin. Let us then approach God's throne of grace with confidence, so that we may receive mercy and find grace to help us in our time of need. (Heb 4:15-16)

> Every high priest is selected from among the people and is appointed to represent the people in matters related to God, to offer gifts and sacrifices for sins. He is able to deal gently with those who are ignorant and are going astray, since he himself is subject to weakness .... During the days of Jesus' life on earth, he

offered up prayers and petitions with fervent
cries and tears to the one who could save him
from death, and he was heard because of his
reverent submission. Son though he was, he
learned obedience from what he suffered and,
once made perfect, he became the source of
eternal salvation for all who obey him. (Heb
5:1-9)

Primarily, Christ took on human form so he could
sacrifice his life on our behalf. Secondly, Christ took on
human form in order to learn and understand our needs
and infirmities, so he can effectively advocate for us in the
court of heaven. Having gone through the same limita-
tions and temptations, he is well equipped to sympathise
and represent us.

6.1.3   He is the sufferer

A third reason for the effectiveness of Christ's intercession is that he was the one who suffered the wages of sins
committed by the very people he is advocating for. The
Scriptures state that the sins of mankind were placed on
Christ as he was sacrificed.

Surely he took up our pain and bore our
suffering, yet we considered him punished by
God, stricken by him, and afflicted. But he
was pierced for our transgressions, he was
crushed for our iniquities; the punishment
that brought us peace was on him, and by
his wounds we are healed. We all, like sheep,
have gone astray, each of us has turned to

our own way; and the LORD has laid on him the iniquity of us all. (Isa 53:4-6)

Christ suffered for you, leaving you an example, that you should follow in his steps ... "He himself bore our sins" in his body on the cross, so that we might die to sins and live for righteousness; "by his wounds you have been healed." (1 Pet 2:21-24)

By virtue of his suffering, he has become an effective advocate for repentant sinners. To some extent, this is similar to the use of victim impact statements in human courts during sentencing hearing. The idea is that the testimony of the victim of a crime is important, and should be considered by the courts when appropriate. In the case of Christ, he speaks for the sinner who has appealed to him for salvation, which is better than speaking for vengeance.[8] This is the reason why the marks of Christ's suffering persisted after the resurrection,[9] to serve as a perpetual reminder of the atonement, and to be used in defence of the sinner in the divine court.

6.2 Interceding for the offender

Just as Christ prays and intercedes for us, he expects us to do the same for those who offend us. Praying for those who offend us represents the final and most God-like step on the journey of forgiveness.

But I tell you, love your enemies and pray for those who persecute you. (Matt 5:44)

[8] Heb 12:24   [9] Luke 24:39

> Bless those who persecute you; bless and
> do not curse. (Rom 12:14)

> Therefore confess your sins to each other
> and pray for each other so that you may be
> healed. The prayer of a righteous person is
> powerful and effective. (James 5:16)

When we pray for those who do us harm, like Christ, our prayers will be effective by virtue of us having suffered from the offence and demonstrating holiness by forgiving the offender. When the victim of an offence genuinely asks God to forgive the perpetrator, they are challenging God on the following basis: if a fallible human can forgive, surely, God, who has no interest in the death of the sinner, can also forgive and bring a willing sinner to repentance. This is a powerful intercessory prayer, the same prayer offered by Christ for those who killed him: "Father, forgive them, for they do not know what they are doing."[10] Stephen also, when he was being murdered, followed the example of Christ and prayed: "Lord, do not hold this sin against them."[11] Anyone who genuinely takes this step and prays for forgiveness on behalf of those who cause them harm has truly followed God and completed the journey of divine forgiveness.

---

[10] Luke 23:34   [11] Acts 7:60

Bibliography

[NIV] Scripture quotations taken from The Holy Bible, New International Version® NIV® Copyright © 1973 1978 1984 2011 by Biblica, Inc.™ Used by permission. All rights reserved worldwide.

[NKJV] Scripture taken from the New King James Version®. Copyright © 1982 by Thomas Nelson. Used by permission. All rights reserved.

[KJV] Scripture taken from The Bible: Authorized King James Version®. Oxford: Oxford University Press. Copyright © 1997 by Carroll, R. P. and Prickett, S. Used by permission. All rights reserved.

[finney] Finney C. G., 1994. Finney's Systematic Theology, Baker Publishing Group.

[dake] Dake F. J., 1999. Dake Annotated Reference Bible, Dake Publishing.

[holman] Butler, T. C. (editor). Entry for "Covenant". Holman Bible Dictionary, 1991. Web address: https://www.studylight.org/dictionaries/eng/hbd/c/covenant.html. Accessed on 14 July 2021.

[timeline] Rich V., 2010. Bible Timeline, Discovery Bible and Biblos.com. Web address: https://biblehub.com /timeline/. Accessed on 15 April 2021.

Glossary

The following are brief definitions of standard words or doctrines, as understood and used by the author in this book.

Accuser: One who brings accusation, charge of crime or offence against another in a court.

Advocate: One who pleads the cause of or defend another in a court.

Atonement: The doctrine of substitutionary death of Christ which allowed God to forgive and save repentant sinners.

Covenant: A pact, treaty, alliance, or agreement between two parties of equal or of unequal authority. [holman]

Faith: The act or process of sinners accepting Christ and surrendering their lives to him for salvation.

Intercessor: One who intervenes (i.e. prays) on behalf of another for forgiveness by God.

Justice: The administration of fair and lawful treatment and equitable retribution.

Justification: The act of God whereby the sinner is pronounced not guilty through repentance and faith in Christ.

Law: A rule of action with sanctions. [finney] Moral law is a rule of voluntary action of the will or intention, as opposed to physical law (i.e. law of necessity). While moral law primarily regulates the intention or the will, human law regulates the outward conduct.

Man: Mankind or the human race, represented by Adam, the first human.

Mediator: One who mediates or makes peace between two parties in conflict.

New Covenant: The covenant God established with mankind through Christ as mediator, based on grace and forgiveness through the atonement of Christ.

Old Covenant: The covenant God established with Israel through Moses as mediator, largely based on principles of vengeance.

Pagan: An unbeliever or a person holding religious beliefs other than Christianity.

Reconciliation: A restoration of the previous relationship destroyed by sin or offence. Reconciliation may be full, partial or impossible (see Section 4.5).

Repentance: The act or process of recognising one's sinfulness and turning to Christ for pardon.

Salvation: The doctrine of deliverance from sin and its consequences, through faith in Christ and his atoning sacrifice.

Sin: Lawlessness or transgression of the law of God (1 John 3:4); a life of nonconformity with the moral requirements of God. A sinner is someone who commits sin or lives a sinful life.

Tax Collector: Literally someone who collects taxes. At the time of Christ, tax collectors for the Roman

government were seen as dishonest, traitors and grouped with
sinners.

the Fall: The transition of Adam and Eve
from a state of innocent obedience
to a state of disobedience and sinfulness.

Vengeance: Revenge or retaliatory action
inflicted on someone for wrong-
doing; especially when motivated
by personal interests or vindictiveness.

Abbreviations

NIV: New International Version
NKJV: New King James Version

Books of the Bible

Gen:	Genesis	2 Chron:	2 Chronicles
Exo:	Exodus	Ezra:	Ezra
Lev:	Leviticus	Neh:	Nehemiah
Num:	Numbers	Esth:	Esther
Deut:	Deuteronomy	Job:	Job
Josh:	Joshua	Psa:	Psalms
Judg:	Judges	Prov:	Proverbs
Ruth:	Ruth	Eccl:	Ecclesiastes
1 Sam:	1 Samuel	Songs:	Songs of Solomon
2 Sam:	2 Samuel	Isa:	Isaiah
1 Kings:	1 Kings	Jer:	Jeremiah
2 Kings:	2 Kings	Lam:	Lamentations
1 Chron:	1 Chronicles	Eze:	Ezekiel

Dan:	Daniel	2 Cor:	2 Corinthians
Hos:	Hosea	Gal:	Galatians
Joel:	Joel	Eph:	Ephesians
Amos:	Amos	Phil:	Philippians
Oba:	Obadiah	Col:	Colossians
Jon:	Jonah	1 Thess:	1 Thessalonians
Mic:	Micah	2 Thess:	2 Thessalonians
Nah:	Nahum	1 Tim:	1 Timothy
Hab:	Habakkuk	2 Tim:	2 Timothy
Zeph:	Zephaniah	Tit:	Titus
Hag:	Haggai	Phile:	Philemon
Zech:	Zechariah	Heb:	Hebrews
Mal:	Malachi	James:	James
Matt:	Matthew	1 Pet:	1 Peter
Mark:	Mark	2 Pet:	2 Peter
Luke:	Luke	1 John:	1 John
John:	John	2 John:	2 John
Acts:	Acts	3 John:	3 John
Rom:	Romans	Jude:	Jude
1 Cor:	1 Corinthians	Rev:	Revelation

About the Author

This book was conceived during the author's role as a Sunday School teacher and lay preacher at Trinity Baptist Church New Addington, London (2016-2018). During this time, the author was assigned a teaching series on Forgiveness—the ideas of this book were preached and refined during the delivery of the series.

By profession, Dr Bright Osei Twumasi is a quantitative risk analyst and a software engineer and holds a PhD in the field. However, he has particular interests in Christian doctrines and philosophy, and has spoken on various topics under those themes.

Milton Keynes UK
Ingram Content Group UK Ltd.
UKHW020804150823
426904UK00016B/657

9 781916 686007